149919

Contemporary
Instrumental
Techniques

Contemporary Instrumental Techniques

by **Gardner Read**

Composer-in-Residence, Boston University

SCHIRMER BOOKS

A Division of Macmillan Publishing Co., Inc.

NEW YORK

Collier Macmillan Publishers

LONDON

1499 19

Schirmer Books
A Division of Macmillan Publishing Co., Inc.
866 Third Avenue, New York, N. Y. 10022

Collier Macmillan Canada, Ltd.

Library of Congress Catalog Card Number: 75-27455

Printed in the United States of America

printing number

1 2 3 4 5 6 7 8 9 10

Library of Congress Cataloging in Publication Data

Read, Gardner
    Contemporary instrumental techniques.

    Bibliography: p.
    Includes indexes.
    1. Instrumental music--Instruction and study.
I. Title.
MT170.R39   785'.07   75-27455
ISBN 0-02-872100-4

CONTENTS

Flutter-tonguing variants. Vibrato. Fingering devices. Breath and air sounds. Mouthpiece and tubing effects. Multiphonics. Vocalizations. Miscellaneous effects. Hybrid instruments.

Tuning of unpitched instruments. New areas of striking. Unusual agents of attack. New methods of striking. Tremoli variants. Idiophone clusters. Miscellaneous effects.

FOREWORD

The author of a compendium on "contemporary instrumental techniques" faces the disconcerting prospect that as soon as his tabulation is published, it is likely to be considered incomplete. For it is a reality of the mid- and late-twentieth century that the "progress" of music has been characterized by an unprecedented and bewildering amount of experimentation with the "techniques" of instruments. Almost every week it seems some composer somewhere is expanding or extending the capacities of traditional instruments. These efforts are often spurred on by attempts to identify with the relatively new sonoric potential of the various forms of electronic media (tape, synthesizer, computer, musique concrète, etc.). Composers are also, whether they are willing to admit it or not, very often inspired by the concept of "noise"—indeed, the *whole* world of sound—as a legitimate means of "musical" expression, first proposed by the Futurists early in the century, and definitely articulated by John Cage in the early 1940's.

To keep pace with these developments in anything approximating a comprehensive manner is an enormous task and amongst American composers there is probably no one more suited to its accomplishment than Gardner Read. A veteran of encyclopedic cataloguing, as brilliantly evidenced in his *Thesaurus of Orchestral Devices*, Mr. Read brings a composer's insights and expertise, a university professor's sense of history, and an experienced compiler's fanatic devotion to encyclopedic comprehensiveness.

Non-musicians would assume that the contents of this book are known to all musicians and composers. Alas, this is far from the truth, and even amongst composers who consider themselves sophisticated avant-gardists, there is at worst a remarkable lack of hard knowledge as to the newest techniques (and their notation), and at best considerable confusion, a factor to be multiplied many times when we come to the average performing musician.

Therefore, for the professional interested in the subject, Gardner Read's new work is of immense value. Indeed, it is a godsend, in that the untold hours of research and plowing through hundreds of scores is readily available in a clear, concise, well structured and handy compendium. And to Mr. Read's credit, it does bring the subject up-to-date—for the moment.

What composers' ingenuity and drive for invention will yield in the future is, of course, hard to foretell. After some 70 years of nearly unrelenting experimentation, often it seemed for experimentation's sake, one might think that the pace would slow a little. And perhaps that is happening. Perhaps we are moving into a period when the innovations of the recent past will be assessed, weighed for their *real* value and long-term durability, and then, hopefully, the residue will be assimilated into the mainstream of compositional creativity. Perhaps even the premise, claimed by some composers, that in the late twentieth century "sound per se is now of primary importance" will also be re-evaluated.

If such evaluations are to take place, they will be made all the easier by Gardner Read's monumental efforts to tell us what in fact we have wrought in the last few decades. For this we are a grateful community of composers, performers, listeners and readers.

—Gunther Schuller

PRELUDE

Composers of the late twentieth century are acutely aware of the bewildering multiplicity of styles and related techniques that are shaping the musical expression of our time. They are in general agreement, however, that sound per se is now of primary importance in the instrumentator's arsenal of techniques. Indeed, contemporary composers en masse have transferred to musical timbre the painter Kandinsky's belief that "Color makes a more insidious attack on the emotions than form."

Whereas self-expression, whether in music, in painting, or in literature, was the paradigm of the nineteenth-century Romantics, musical means have now become more important and more relevant to composers than artistic ends. Compositional and instrumental techniques exist today for their own intrinsic sakes rather than serving, as they did in the past, as vehicles of highly personalized sentiment.

A significant development and refinement of instrumental potential has taken place during recent years. Effects undreamed of, or once thought impossible by the early twentieth-century orchestrators, are now commonplaces in the vanguard scores of the present day; yet not all composers are fully aware of these developments nor of their pervasive influence on the kinds of music now being composed. Some instrumental techniques are understood only dimly or are utilized only tentatively, if at all. Indeed, certain new instrumentational devices are widely misunderstood, both as to the physical procedures involved and the results in terms of sound.

It is, therefore, the primary purpose of this compendium to codify these techniques, to explain their production in terms of idiomatic peculiarity and limitation, and to cite representative scores in which the new devices form an integral part of the composer's sonoric concepts. Its immanent value does not depend, of course, upon the prolific citation of bizarre instrumental effects—

often more interesting as notations than as sounds—but on the systematic and detailed codification of modern instrumental potentiality. How, and under what compositional circumstances or in what stylistic context these techniques can be most felicitous, are decisions every composer must make for himself.

Even thoroughly experienced composers are sometimes apt to forget that their performers are not robots; they are human beings with human limitations of physical endowment and perception. If the avant-gardist is frequently impatient with these limitations, his solution is to create his music solely for the tape recorder, which knows no limitations other than its source of power. But if the composer utilizes conventional instruments played by human beings, he should not demand the physically impossible but only the realistically attainable from his performers.

All composers, whether experimental or basically conservative, deal with commonly shared materials—tonal, rhythmic, timbral, and formalistic. But no modern materials available to the contemporary orchestrator, it is safe to assert, are more fruitful than the current expansion of instrumental capability. Perhaps in the pages to follow both the composer and the performer may find as yet unexplored means towards the achievement of their common artistic ends as well as some unsuspected insights into modern instrumental potentiality.

LIST OF EXAMPLES

Part I

Generalized

Techniques

INTRODUCTION

Many so-called "new" instrumental devices have developed from well-established techniques; they are extensions of, or refinements of, procedures long considered part of a composer's repertorium of expressive devices. The newness, then, is not one of kind but of degree, a further and more extensive development of basic effects found in scores from the late nineteenth century to the present day. Muting, glissandi, harmonics, and even certain percussive devices (as applied to nonpercussion instruments) are instrumental techniques common to the late Romantics (Mahler, in particular), the Impressionists (primarily Debussy and, to a lesser extent, Ravel), the Expressionists (beginning with Schoenberg, Berg, and Webern), and most certainly including the Neo-Romantics (Prokofiev, Bartók, and Britten, to name a few outstanding representatives).

More patently new, in conception and in method of individual production, are the techniques of microtones and of sound amplification, the latter applied to conventional instruments in live performance rather than referring to electronic composition. Newest and most radical in artistic conceptualization are the diverse theatrical effects now demanded of the instrumentalist (and vocalist, too)—extramusical devices injected to enhance the composer's avant-gardism.

Because all of the foregoing devices apply to all kinds of instruments, they are considered in Part I as generalized procedures that with but slight modification apply to all orchestral or ensemble members. In Part II the new devices and instrumentational techniques discussed are exclusively idiomatic in nature; that is, they are conditioned by the individual constructions, basic performance procedures, and inherent limitations of the separate instruments. The effects catalogued are thus confined to similarities of instrumental type or family: flutter-tonguing, for example, is a unique wind-instrument technique and cannot be achieved on percussion, keyboard, and stringed instruments; mechanical pedal effects are possible only on harp and certain keyboard instruments; similarly, *sul ponticello* is a manner of playing restricted to the bowed strings, and so on.

The order of instrumental discussion in each section of Parts I and II, whether inter- or intra-choir, is always according to the traditional vertical format of the printed orchestral score page: woodwinds first, then brasses, followed by percussion, harp and other plucked instruments, keyboard instruments, and ending with the strings. And within each choir the instruments are generally referred to in similar verticality, according to their normal contiguous positions on the score page.

Purely in the interests of space, references to a composer's works in the many sectional listings throughout the book have been restricted to two citations; if other scores by the same composer also illustrate the technique under discussion, it is so stated.

The choice of any particular work for citation or for illustration was governed by two criteria: 1) the clear and unequivocal demonstration of the instrumental or coloristic technique being analyzed, and 2) the availability of the score. Few manuscripts have been included and these only when they presented "one-of-a-kind" technical demonstrations or were otherwise unique in their utilization of the established devices.

The majority of the quoted musical examples serve a multiple purpose: that is, they frequently illustrate more than one unusual technical or expressive device. Hence the reader will often find cross-references to one or another of the score illustrations in chapters and sections other than those in which the examples are placed.

It should be evident that, of necessity, a rather rigorous and self-imposed selectivity resulted in a modest number of significant musical illustrations rather than a plethora of more routine examples that would serve a less useful purpose.

Because the primary focus of the book is on instrumental performance techniques, purely compositional or stylistic concepts are referred to, if at all, only peripherally. Consequently, there is no discussion here of aleatoric music, nor of improvisation, nor of formalistic considerations, except as they impinge directly on the performing techniques and the all-important parameter of tone color.

Although this survey of new instrumental devices was not designed expressly to be a textbook of contemporary orchestration, it could advantageously serve that purpose. It might also be profitably utilized as supplementary reference material in courses of basic instrumentation and of advanced composition and analysis. Performers, too, will find herein information regarding novel playing effects on their instruments not generally available elsewhere— certainly not within the confines of a single volume.

The multiplicity of new and experimental instrumental techniques has been equaled, if not surpassed, by a corresponding proliferation of new instrumental symbology. Because a consensus among composers and performers on the new notations is conspicuously lacking, it seemed inadvisable to include detailed discussion regarding the best choice among the existing notations. Just as each composer must determine subjectively the compositional and stylistic feasibility of any technique described in this book so must he make a subjective choice among the concomitant symbologies currently in use.

1

EXTENDED RANGES

In the phenomenal development of late twentieth-century instrumental techniques it was inevitable that the total range of many of the orchestral and band instruments would be extended. Although these extensions are certainly not available to all instrumentalists, they form an important segment of modern instrumental potentiality. Range extensions are made possible by several means: first, by mechanical resources—longer tubing and extra keys on wind instruments; larger models of tuned percussion members; lengthened strings or the employment of scordatura on stringed instruments, and so on; second, by the development of individual performer technique.

Woodwinds

Among the woodwind instruments whose ranges have now been notably increased, the flute has for many years been enabled to sound a low B by means of an extra key,[1] and to sound pitches higher than d^4, formerly considered the uppermost limit of the instrument. By means of embouchure manipulation and

[1]Possibly the earliest example of low B occurs in the *Intermezzo* of Mendelssohn's incidental music to *A Midsummer Night's Dream* (1843).

diaphragm control, certain flutists have recently been able to extend this limit to f⁴—even on rare occasions to f♯⁴, though the quality of sound is predictably rough and breathy. On the other hand, e⁴ is both "safe" and of acceptable quality. For examples of the altissimo register see:

P. Boulez: *Sonatine pour Flûte*
A. Gilbert: *The Incredible Flute Music*
J. Heiss: *Movements for Three Flutes*
J. Mekeel: *The Shape of Silence*
C. Wuorinen: *Flute Variations*

A normally blown low B♭ is now possible by pulling out the head-joint about an inch and fingering low B. Thus the several B♭'s in three of Mahler's symphonies and the one in Ravel's orchestration of the Mussorgsky *Pictures at an Exhibition* (see page 139 of the pocket score) can no longer be regarded as notational errors.

Stokes and Condon maintain that the flute range can be extended downward by an octave (from c¹) through the use of so-called subtones;[2] that is, buzzing with the lips into the aperture as though it were a brass mouthpiece. They also suggest stopping the open end of the flute with a cork or pressing it against the player's leg to produce a soft pitch one octave lower than the blown note.

Key slaps, although primarily a percussive device (see pp. 61–63), can also lower the pitches fingered into the octave below the instrument's normal range. Vigorously slapping the G-key with the left-hand fourth finger, while at the same time covering the blowhole with the tongue or the chin and fingering any one of the pitches from b to a♯¹ with the right hand, results in a percussive tone a major seventh below the fingered note. This effect was used successfully by:

D. Harris: *Ludus II*
J. Heiss: *Movements for Three Flutes*[3]
B. Levy: *Orbs with Flute*
C. Polin: *The Death of Procris* (Example 1)

George Crumb instructs the alto flute player in *Night of the Four Moons* to cover the air hole with the mouth while clicking the keys of certain specified pitches to produce tones an *octave* lower than notated. Anthony Gilbert includes

[2]See Bibliography, page 233.
[3]Refer to this composer's several articles on flute techniques in *Perspectives of New Music* (Bibliography, page 232).

Example 1   Claire Polin: from *The Death of Procris* (p. 8)

clicks on flute yield: 1. natural fingerings indicated = true pitch

2. covered embouchure hole by lip, indicated = finger; = pitch.

© Copyright 1973 by Seesaw Music Corp., New York. Reproduced by permission.

a parallel directive in his *The Incredible Flute Music:* "Block head-joint hole with tongue and finger energetically an 8va above notated pitch."

Under normal circumstances it is not possible to lower the bottom B♭ of the oboe, but Barney Childs in his *Nonet* tells the player to insert a long cardboard tube in the bell and use the B♭-fingering; the resultant pitch is indeterminately lower than B♭ and is extremely rough and blatant. At the opposite end of the range, high B♭, B, and C are now available to certain oboists, the result of special fingerings and an ultratight embouchure.

Low C on clarinet,[4] A_1 and G_1 on basson, and A_2 on contrabasson are achieved mechanically by means of cardboard tubing or a rolled cylinder of stiff drawing paper, about a foot in length, inserted into the bell of the instrument. Refer to the following scores:

P. Chihara: *Branches* (Example 14)
D. Erb: *Symphony of Overtures*
G. Ligeti: *Requiem*
D. Martino: *B,A,B,B,IT,T* (Example 2)
I. Stravinsky: *Chant du Rossignol; Symphony in C*

[4]All note references are at concert pitch.

In Donald Martino's solo clarinet work listed above, nine cylinders of different lengths are required at various times to enable the player to lower drastically the normal range of the instrument, the nadir being B♭ below the bass staff. According to the composer, the instrument bell is to be removed and the cylinders inserted into the end-joint as needed, held in position with masking tape.

The bass clarinet in William Albright's *Danse Macabre* is given a low C, achieved by pulling out the instrument neck a half-step and fingering D. Even lower pitches, however, have been requisitioned by other composers, most notably by:

Example 2   Donald Martino: from *B,A,B,B,IT,T* (p. 5)

© Copyright 1970 by Ione Press; permission to reprint granted by sole agent: E. C. Schirmer Music Company, Boston.

R. R. Bennett: *Commedia I* (B_1, B♮)
L. Janáĉek: *Sinfonietta* (B_1, B♭, A_1, A♮, G♭, F_1)
A. Khachaturian: *Gayne Ballet Suite; Piano Concerto* (B_1, B♭)
W. Piston: *Second Symphony* (B_1, B♮ A_1, A♮)
D. Shostakovich: *Symphonies No. 6, 7, 11* (B_1)

Presumably these composers had especially constructed instruments in mind or else the players resorted to mechanical extensions to produce such subterranean pitches.

The upper ranges of the several saxophones have now been extended by a full octave and the lower ranges by a minor second.[5] On the baritone saxophone an added whole-step below the normally available low concert D♭ is attainable by placing a specially designed cone in the instrument bell. Though the use of this device slightly dampens the resonance, it does provide a welcome extension to the bottom area of the instrument.

Pitches higher than the conventional limits of English horn, clarinet, and bass clarinet are achieved by ultratight embouchure and/or unusual fingerings worked out by the individual player; hence they vary in quality according to the performer's ability. On bassoon, pitches above e^2 require almost superhuman lip control; predictably, they appear sparingly even in contemporary scores. In all such instances, intonation is shaky, tone quality is strained and rough, and pitch is frequently approximate rather than precise. If these conditions can be regarded as desirable from the vanguardist's point of view, however, there is no reason why they cannot be exploited in his works.

Brasses

As with woodwinds, extended ranges in the brass instruments are accomplished through combinations of embouchure control and special fingerings. Although f^2 should still be regarded as the highest feasible pitch available to the average hornist, some players can achieve up to a b♭^{2}, but only at a relatively high dynamic level. In point of fact, none of the brasses can exceed their normal upper limits at a moderate amplitude, nor without a progressive loss of stable intonation.

Both trumpet and trombone are now frequently required to exceed their traditional upper frequency boundaries. One cannot assign a precise and fixed limit for these stratospheric pitches; it depends almost wholly upon the individ-

---

[5]See *The Art of Saxophone Playing* by Larry Teal (Bibliography, page 233) for fingering charts.

ual player's embouchure and breath control. Certain jazz trumpeters can reach c^4 without undue difficulty, and bb^2 is available to skilled trombonists. Beyond these demonstrated possibilities, however, lies *terra incognita*.

The lower ranges of all the brass instruments have likewise been extended. The horn can now descend to G_1, as in Ligeti's *Ten Pieces for Wind Quintet,* though the tonal quality is quite rough. To enable his trumpet player to go lower than the conventional f♯ or e, Barney Childs in *Nonet* instructs the player to insert a cardboard tube in the bell. Pedal tones (down to E_1) have been required of trombonists since the early part of the twentieth century, but composers must remember that the sound quality of these notes is far less focused than for those low pitches available by means of the modern F-attachment. As for tuba, although both ends of its total range have been somewhat extended, no specific boundary-notes can be cited; they vary according to individual performer techniques. Whereas bb^1 is available to most players, even higher pitches can be obtained by certain virtuoso performers on the instrument.

Percussion

Among the pitched membranophones whose compasses can be mechanically enlarged, the timpani can now achieve tones on the plastic-headed drums somewhat beyond the traditional limits dictated by the older membrane-covered drum heads (see Example 12). These extreme pitches, however, are rather unreliable in intonation and of dubious quality.

Newcomers to the percussion section are the Roto-toms—a set of mounted tom-toms (usually up to five) which can be tuned like timpani to specific pitches. They may, as a consequence, be considered as extensions of the timpani in a higher range, a fact that greatly enlarges the instrumentator's tuned percussive resources.

Extended ranges on the keyed idiophones are entirely a matter of physical construction. That is, pitches higher or lower than those given in standard orchestration manuals as normal limits are available only on larger models of glockenspiel, xylophone, vibraphone, or marimba. Inasmuch as such nonstandard models are not everywhere available, idiophone range extensions cannot yet be regarded as feasible by contemporary orchestrators.

Harp and Other Plucked Instruments

The harp, guitar, and mandolin can have their extreme ranges enlarged only by means of scordatura. The highest string of these instruments can be

tuned up a half—at the very most, a whole—scale-degree, and their lowest
string tuned down by no more than a major second, possibly a minor third. To
raise a string higher would be to risk breaking it, and to slacken a string further
would be to deprive it of resonance and hence of specific pitch. Both Alban
Berg's opera *Wozzeck* and Maurice Ravel's ballet *Daphnis et Chloé*, as well as
the more recent cello concerto of György Ligeti, offer instances of low B♭ for
the harp achieved by pretuning the bottom C-string, as the pedal mechanism
does not affect this string.

Strings

Extending the upper ranges of the various stringed instruments is almost
entirely a matter of the performer's ability; it requires playing in an exceedingly
high position, with fingers cramped together, and with little room on the string
to maneuver. Intonation is invariably wobbly and tones are tense and strained;
yet these sounds are considered viable and are deliberately exploited in much
experimental composition today. Rather than specify actual pitches in the
stratospheric positions, many composers have adopted the device of merely
calling for the highest pitch(es) the player is capable of producing. Notationally,
this is now quite generally indicated with a solid arrowhead or ×-shaped notehead placed somewhat above the staff (Example 39, page 216).

As far as the lower ranges of all the strings are concerned, extensions are
accomplished by means of the time-honored device of scordatura. Violins and
violas are seldom required to lower their fourth strings by more than a whole-
step; in Arnold Bax's *First Symphony*, for instance, the violins' G-string is
lowered to F and the solo viola's C-string to B. However, Iannis Xenakis, in his
ST/4-1, 080262 for string quartet, requires the violist to lower the C-string by a
perfect fourth (Example 3). Cellos and doublebasses in several recent vanguard
scores have had to exceed even that more radical scordatura: in both William
Albright's *Danse Macabre* and the Xenakis work just mentioned (Example 3),
the cellists must tune their C-strings down a full octave. In a number of
experimental Polish scores, including Penderecki's *Fluorescences* (Example
11), the doublebasses are asked to lower the pitch of their bottom string as far as
possible. In *Strobo I* by Alcides Lanza the two lowest doublebass strings are to
be similarly pretuned, while the two highest strings are to be raised in pitch as
far as possible. When the bottom string(s) of either the cello or the doublebass is
lowered to the point of complete slackness, obviously the sound produced is only
approximate in pitch; what comes out in performance is more of an indistinct
rumble than a clear musical tone.

Example 3   Iannis Xenakis: from *ST/4-1, 080262* (p. 16)

Further extensions of certain instrumental ranges may well be feasible, yet there surely must be a physical limit beyond which frequency increments cannot be successfully attained. Even now the expansions of instrumental pitch boundaries have in some instances entered the realm of "white noise"—valid in its own right but limited in its relevance to recognizable pitch distinction. It would seem that the law of diminishing returns would operate decisively in curtailing further significant range expansion—at least among traditional instruments. For new or for hybrid instruments the problem of increasing their total gamut may perhaps be solved more satisfactorily.

2

MUTING

Woodwinds and Brasses

Whereas the muting of a brass instrument in contemporary music is almost too common to warrant mention, the device is encountered far more rarely in parts for woodwind instruments—and for good reason. More effective in theory than in practice, woodwind muting is limited in application and only moderately successful as a timbral agent. The basic reason is that the tube opening or bell of the instrument is not the sole avenue of blown sound; to close the bell artificially affects only a relatively few pitches at the lower end of the instrument range.

The flute and alto flute may be partially muted by inserting a piece of soft tissue or cloth in the tubing after removing the foot-joint, but only c^1 and $c\sharp^1$ are slightly affected. Somewhat higher pitches can be muted by employing the technique of spread tones. These are delicate alterations of normal timbre accomplished by closing the finger holes below the one open hole which produces the required pitch; they may be used to "mute" the tones from $d\sharp^1$ to $a\sharp^1$. Spread tones are actually more successful as a muting device than the artificial, and limited, closing of the tube end.

Stokes and Condon, in their *Special Effects for Flute*,[1] suggest muting the instrument with a piece of masking tape partially covering the embouchure

[1]See Bibliography, page 233.

hole. The muting is thus achieved by reducing the air flow rather than by blocking its egress as a specific tone.

The remaining woodwind instruments may have a cloth, wadded-up handkerchief, or large cork stuffed into the bell, but again only a few low notes on each of the instruments are affected by this muting device. In György Ligeti's *Lontano* the contrabassoon is muffled with a horn mute that is to be placed in the tube end by the player seated next to the contrabassoonist. In the *Sinfonia N. 6* of Hans Werner Henze the saxophone is briefly muted, presumably with a specially designed ring, looking like an oversized doughnut and covered with velvet ribbon. Its primary advantage over a cloth or cork mute is that the bell tones (the lowest three pitches) can still be sounded when the instrument is muted with this agent.

The instruments listed below are to be muted with pieces of cloth or, in a few instances, with corks or felt plugs:

Oboe and/or English horn:

P. Boulez: *Éclat*

K. Huber: *Tenebrae*

D. Martino: *Cinq Frammenti*

P. Méfano: *Interférences*

R. Reynolds: *Quick are the Mouths of Earth*

K. Stockhausen: *Adieu*

I. Stravinsky: *Petrouchka*

W. Szalonek: *Aarhus Music*

A. de la Vega: *Exospheres for Oboe and Piano*

Clarinet and/or bass clarinet:

W. Szalonek: *Aarhus Music*

A. de la Vega: *Interpolation for Solo Clarinet*

Saxophone:

C. Delvincourt: *Pamir*

J. Fortner: *S pr ING*

S. Hodkinson: *Interplay*

Bassoon and/or contrabassoon:

C. Ballif: *Voyage de mon oreille*

K. Huber: *Tenebrae*

G. Ligeti: *Lontano; Requiem,* and other works

K. Stockhausen: *Adieu*

W. Szalonek: *Aarhus Music*

An interesting simulation of muting is requested of the oboist in Szalonek's *Les Sons:* the player is to enclose the mouthpiece (staple) tightly with the clenched fist, gradually unclenching the hand during playing. The woodwind equivalent of brass instrument stopped-open (+ −0) procedures, the same technique is to be applied to oboe, English horn, and bassoon in Donald Erb's *The Seventh Trumpet.*

More feasible on brass than on woodwind instruments is the device of inserting a mute gradually in the bell of the instrument while playing. The effect, possible on all the brasses save tuba, and analogous to gradual hand-stopping on the horn, has been requested by:

H. W. Henze: *4. Sinfonie*
H. Holliger: *Siebengesang*
G. Rochberg: *Tableaux*

Conversely, the mute may be removed gradually from the bell, just as the hornist's clenched hand may be slowly withdrawn from inside the bell; see:

D. Bedford: *Pentomino*
E. Brown: *Available Forms 2*
N. T. Dao: *Phū-Dồng*
D. Erb: *Concerto for Solo Percussionist*
T. Ichiyanagi: *Activities*
L. de Pablo: *Modulos III*
E. Schwartz: *Essays; Rip,* and other works
K. Serocki: *Symphonic Frescoes*
K. Stockhausen: *Punkte*

A related effect is obtainable on trombone by rapidly opening or closing a plunger mute in the bell:

D. Bedford: *Trona*
L. Berio: *Sequenza V*
J. Druckman: *Animus 1* (Example 29)
V. Globokar: *Accord; Discours II,* and other works
W. Heider: *-einander*
J. Heinke: *Music for Trombone and Percussion*

The requisition of different types of brass mutes in modern scores is too prevalent to warrant further discussion.[2] It might be of interest, however, to mention several recent substitutes for less commonly available mute types. For example, Michael Colgrass in *As Quiet As* suggests that a harmon mute with a piece of felt stuffed in the pinhole would be an acceptable surrogate for "whisper" mute. Similarly, Gunther Schuller in *Study in Textures* requests his brass players to cover their cup mutes with a cloth to simulate solotone mutes. And Barbara Kolb tells her trombonists in *Trobar Clus* to use a cup mute with extra felt if bucket mutes are not available. In *Remembrances* Lawrence Moss asks that a cup mute be further softened by winding a handkerchief around the cup before inserting it in the instrument bell.

Of the more commonly available mute types, the tone of a harmon mute can be variously altered by pulling out the stem, by degrees or completely (as required in *Éclat* of Pierre Boulez and in Schuller's *Study in Textures,* for example).

Feasible and highly effective, though strangely not a conspicuous requisition in contemporary scores, is the simultaneous use by similar brass instruments of different mute types. In his *Sinfonia,* for instance, Berio requires one trumpet to use plunger mute, one to use harmon mute, and two others to employ straight mutes—all playing concurrently. And in *Epifanie* four trumpets synchronistically employ wa-wa, cup, straight, and plunger mutes—a fascinating amalgam of muted brass tone. (See also Jacob Druckman's *Windows* and Donald Erb's *The Seventh Trumpet.*)

Rather exotic mute substitutes have on occasion been designated by certain avant-gardists: for example, in both *Apparitions* and *Aventures* Ligeti asks that the horn be muted with a cloth stuffed tightly into the bell (also required of trumpet in the *Double Concerto for ondes Martenot, Percussion and Orchestra* of Josep Mestres-Quadreny). Furthermore, Ligeti directs (in *Aventures*) that the hornist also use a large round vase with a narrow neck for muting purposes; he does not, however, explain how the vase is to be made secure in the bell opening. One presumes that it must be held in place with the hand, somewhat awkward for the player.

A muting trick borrowed from early jazz performance technique is to muffle the open tones of trumpet and trombone by playing directly into the music stand, the bell held as close as possible in front of the music on the rack (as in Merrill Ellis's *Mutations* and Paul Méfano's *Paraboles*).

---

[2]Refer to the author's *Thesaurus of Orchestral Devices* for a listing of generally available mute types and references to scores that require each kind.

Percussion

Muting is a technical and timbral device that would not seem to have much relevance when applied to percussion instruments, but this is not the case. The various membranophones, timpani and tuned drums included, can all be muted in at least two different ways. First, a piece of cloth, a folded handkerchief, or a felt pad may be laid on the drum surface to muffle its normal resonance:

J. Cage: *First Construction (in Metal)*
M. Colgrass: *As Quiet As*
H. Ebenhöh: *4 Szenen für 10*
S. Hodkinson: *Imagind Quarter*
M. Kagel: *Anagrama*
L. Kupkovik: *Das Fleisch des kreuzes*
J. M. Mestres-Quadreny: *Tramesa a Tapies*
G. Read: *Los Dioses Aztecas*
W. Russell: *Fugue for Eight Percussion Instruments*
D. Shostakovich: *Violin Concerto*
B. A. Zimmermann: *Canto di speranza*

In Walter Ross's trombone concerto, one timpano is muted by laying the protective cardboard cover on the head; this is struck with a bass drum beater instead of with normal timpani mallets. In *Windows* Jacob Druckman mutes a timpano by asking the player to lay a cymbal, rim down, on the surface.

For the second manner of muting, the flat hand or spread fingers are pressed against the membrane before striking, so as to deaden the normal vibration of the drumhead:

D. Bedford: *Piece for Mo*
P. Boulez: *Le marteau sans maître*
E. Carter: *Eight Pieces for Four Timpani*
V. Globokar: *Voie*
H-J. Hespos: *Passagen*
M. Kagel: *Anagrama; Sonant*
R. Reynolds: *Quick are the Mouths of Earth*
Z. Rudzinski: *Impromptu for Orchestra; Moments musicaux II*
W. Russell: *Fugue for Eight Percussion Instruments*
W. Schuman: *Symphony No. 7*
K. Serocki: *Episodes; Musica concertante*
B. A. Zimmermann: *Canto di speranza*

A snare drum may, in addition, be muted by laying a cloth or handkerchief on the snares themselves, with the drum turned upside down (required in Kagel's *Anagrama*).

Pitched mallet instruments—marimba, xylophone, vibraphone, and glockenspiel—can be effectively muted by pressing the fingers of one hand on the bars while striking with a mallet in the other; these requirements appear in:

P. Boulez: *Le marteau sans maître*
S. Hodkinson: *Fresco; Imagind Quarter*
J. McKenzie: *Paths I*
Y. Sadai: *Nuances*
B. Schäffer: *Scultura*

These instruments may also be muted by the player laying a cloth or felt pad, even a folded handkerchief, on the plates to be struck, as designated in:

N. T. Dao: *Máy*
G. Heussenstamm: *Seventeen Impressions*
K. Huber: *Tenebrae*
B. Maderna: *III Concerto per Oboe*

A percussionist mutes chimes and triangle by grasping the metal tubing or bar with one hand, while playing with the other:

P. Boulez: *Le marteau sans maître*
N. Castiglioni: *A Solemn Music II*
M. Kagel: *Anagrama*
G. Read: *Los Dioses Aztecas*
W. Russell: *Fugue for Eight Percussion Instruments*
W. Schuman: *Credendum*
K. Serocki: *Continuum; Episodes*

Suspended cymbals, gongs, and tam-tams are customarily muted by holding their edges between the fingers of one hand, while playing on the surface with some agent in the other hand:

D. Bedford: *Piece for Mo*
H. Birtwistle: *Nomos*
L. Foss: *Echoi; Fragments of Archilochos*
M. Kagel: *Anagrama*

W. Russell: *Three Dance Movements*
W. Schuman: *Symphony No. 7*
T. Sikorski: *Echa II*

In William Hellermann's *Formata* the suspended cymbal is to be muffled by laying or taping a piece of paper on the cymbal surface. A similar effect is obtained in the *Tramesa a Tapies* of Mestres-Quadreny by draping a cloth over the cymbal. Several composers have called for gongs to be muted by laying them flat on a large pad (or blanket) spread on the floor or a table and then striking them; this stipulation appears in Cage's *First Construction (in Metal)* and in Henry Cowell's *Set of Five*.

Maracas can be dampened in sound by holding them by the heads rather than by the handles when shaking or rotating them; both Anthony Gilbert in his *Introit, Gradual and Two Chorals* and Kagel in *Anagrama* request this action. Finally, cowbells may be muffled by stuffing a cloth into their openings.

Orchestrators should be reminded that none of the foregoing muted effects should be confused with ordinary muffling of the vibrations of a percussion instrument after it has been struck.

Harp

Hand muffling of the harp strings is a routine performance technique and therefore does not constitute a bona fide muting device. Nor are "isolated sounds" and "xyloharmonic sounds" (so named by the French composer-harpist Carlos Salzedo) genuine muting effects. "Isolated sounds" result from muffling a string at the precise moment of plucking the next string required, and "xyloharmonic sounds" are the immediate muffling of harmonics. Properly qualified as harp string muting is the technique of muffling the string at the actual moment of plucking it. One such procedure is Salzedo's "snare drum effect": the left hand is laid flat along the tops of a limited number of strings near the tuning pins while the right hand plays so-called "gushing chords" (see page 37). Many of Salzedo's solo harp pieces call for this effect, as do the following works:

L. Berio: *Sequenza II* (Example 4-d)
J. Druckman: *Windows*
V. Globokar: *Voie*
M. D. Levy: *Kyros*
V. Persichetti: *Sinfonia: Janiculum*
J. Serebrier: *Colores Magicos*
T. Takemitsu: *Eucalypts (I)*

Another, and closely related, effect entails dampening a single string with a finger of one hand—or a group of contiguous strings with the flat hand—close to the soundboard while playing with the other hand in normal position. This effect, termed "xylophonic sounds" in the Salzedo lexicon, appears in the following scores:

L. Berio: *Circles; Sequenza II* (Example 4-a)
P. Boulez: *Le Soleil des Eaux*
V. Globokar: *Voie*
H. Holliger: *Glühende Rätsel*
B..Jolas: *Tranche*
M. Kagel: *Anagrama; Sonant* (Example 9-c)
W. Kotonski: *Concerto per quattro*
B. Rands: *Formants I*
C. Salzedo: *Sonata for Harp*

Conversely, the harp strings can be muffled at their midpoint and plucked near to the soundboard, *a la guitarra:*

L. Berio: *Chemins I; Sequenza II* (Example 4-e)
B. Rands: *Formants I*
T. Takemitsu: *Eucalypts (I)*

A harp string may also be dampened with the fingernail pressed against it; when the string is plucked by the other hand, it vibrates against the nail, producing a faint metallic "buzz." This technique is required in:

S. Bussotti: *Fragmentations; Memoria,* and other works
M. Kagel: *Sonant*
B. Rands: *Formants I*
I. Xenakis: *ST/10-1, 080262*

Donald Erb (in *Symphony of Overtures*) requires the harpist to hold a tuning fork against a vibrating string, while in *Sonant* (Example 9-t) Kagel calls for a drumstick and a triangle beater to be similarly employed.

In the same work Kagel asks that the strings be dampened with the player's whole arm, laid flat, while the other hand is engaged in playing. In Heinz Holliger's *Siebengesang* the harpist muffles the strings with his flat left hand while sliding across the strings with a plectrum in the right hand. In Gilbert Amy's *Trajectoires* the player dampens the strings with the palm while striking them with a triangle beater.

Example 4   Luciano Berio: from *Sequenza II* (p. 4)

Qualifying as a muted effect are the "vibrant sounds" invented by Salzedo: the left thumb presses firmly against the string just below the tuning pins while the right hand plucks the string. The composer's notation shown below has not been improved upon:

In addition to the muting procedures just discussed, the normal timbre of the harp can be altered by threading a piece of tissue paper (about ³⁄₄″ wide) or a thin ribbon through the plastic strings. The tone thus created is remarkably akin to that of the harpsichord or, less obviously perhaps, of the lute. This type of muting is required in Bussotti's *Fragmentations*, in George Crumb's *Ancient Voices of Children*, and in Edgard Varèse's *Ameriques*.

Keyboard Instruments

Of the several keyboard instruments, only the piano and the harpsichord can be mechanically muted so as to alter the natural sound of the instrument. There are several ways in which the alteration of piano tone-color can be accomplished: first, the pianist dampens the string(s) with the fingertips or the palm of one hand while playing on the keys with the other hand. By means of varying pressures on the string the sound can be further modified: a very light finger pressure changes the tone minimally, while a firm and heavy pressure results in a dead, thudding tone ("bass drum effect" on the very lowest strings). There are far too many contemporary works utilizing these muting procedures to justify a complete individual listing, but a few might be mentioned:

E. Brown: *Hodograph I; Music for Cello and Piano*
D. Burge: *Aeolian Music*
S. Bussotti: *Couple; Il Nudo,* and other works
J. Cage: *Concert for Piano and Orchestra*
S. Cervetti: *Five Episodes; Six Sequences*
B. Childs: *Jack's New Bag*
G. Crumb: *Echoes of Time and the River; Eleven Echoes of Autumn,* and other works
L. Foss: *Echoi*
M. Kagel: *Anagrama*
W. Kotonski: *Pour quatre*
A. Lanza: *Acúfenos I*

H. Lazarof: *Textures*
B. Maderna: *Oboe Concerto*
H. Pousseur: *Honeyrêves*
B. Rands: *Espressione IV; Wildtrack 1*
R. Reynolds: *Blind Men; The Emperor of Ice Cream*
E. Schwartz: *Music for Prince Albert*

Composers have often requested a gradual increase or decrease of finger pressure on the string while the key is being depressed (as in Gilbert's *Sonata No. 2*). Not infrequently they have specified exact areas of the strings where the fingers or flat hand are to be placed:

1. At the end of the string
   J. Cage: *Pastorale for Piano Solo*
   G. Crumb: *Echoes of Time and the River; Makrokosmos—Vol. I*

2. Near the pinboard (pegs, nut)
   W. Albright: *Pianoagogo*
   D. Burge: *Aeolian Music*
   G. Crumb: *Eleven Echoes of Autumn*
   H. Hartwell: *Soul Piece*

3. Close to the dampers
   M. Finnissy: *As When Upon a Tranced Summer Night*
   A. Lanza: *Plectros II*

4. Between the hammers (dampers) and the pegs (pinboard)
   D. Cope: *Parallax*
   D. Erb: *The Seventh Trumpet*

5. Near the bridge
   E. Brown: *From Here*
   F. Cerha: *Spiegel II*
   Chou Wen-chung: *Cursive*
   W. Hellermann: *Formata*
   R. Reynolds: *Mosaic; Quick are the Mouths of Earth,* and other works

A piano string (or series of contiguous strings) can also be finger-muted *after* the key has been depressed, or struck with the sustaining pedal held down (as in William Albright's *Pianoagogo*, Kagel's *Anagrama* and Joel Spiegelman's *Morsels*). In Christian Wolff's *Duet I* the composer asks that the pianist mute a certain string with his finger but at the same time allow the fingernail to lightly touch an adjacent string; when the key of this string is struck, the resulting vibration against the nail creates a delicate buzzing.

Muting the piano strings in a somewhat different manner is accomplished by preperformance preparation: the player inserts such objects as screws, bolts, nuts, nails, erasers or rubber wedges, paper clips, pencils, coins, and the like, between certain preselected strings. John Cage, of course, is the uncontested pioneer in the field of "prepared piano" (in *Amores* and other early pieces).[3] Later composers, including those listed below, have been quick to adapt the technique to their own peculiar requirements:

> L. Austin: *Accidents*
> Z. Bargielski: *Parades*
> D. Bedford: *Piano Piece 2*
> B. Childs: *Jack's New Bag*
> L. Hiller: *Machine Music*

[3]A comprehensive and amply illustrated discussion of piano interior preparation will be found in Richard Bunger's *The Well-Prepared Piano* (see Bibliography, page 232).

Example 5   Toshiro Mayuzumi: from *Pieces for Prepared Piano and Strings* (p. 3)

*)
Place two pieces of rubber in each of the following strings:

**)
Place two little bolts without nuts or small screws in each of the following strings:

***)
Place a large screw in each of the following strings:

T. Mayuzumi: *Pieces for Prepared Piano and Strings* (Example 5)
E. Schwartz: *Music for Napoleon and Beethoven; Soliloquies*
C. Wolff: *Suite I*

A curious effect: at one point in Hiller's work a rubber band is to be tied around several of the low strings, thus muting them when the corresponding keys are struck; at the same time, one hand stretches the rubber band and lets it snap against the strings, creating an explosive crack.

Any piano string, or group of strings, can also be muted by placing various objects on top of the string(s). The following list is testimony to the vanguardist's sonic imagination:

1. A pad or soft cloth, such as a wadded-up handkerchief

    A. Gilbert: *Sonata No. 2*
    G. Ligeti: *Nouvelles Aventures*

2. A thick towel

    A. Janson: *Canon*

3. A felt or rubber mat

    M. Kagel: *Transición* II

4. A strip of paper or cardboard[4]

    A. Gilbert: *Sonata No. 2*
    R. Reynolds: *The Emperor of Ice Cream*

5. A strip (or several strips) of adhesive or masking tape

    D. Erb: *The Seventh Trumpet*
    W. Szalonek: *Proporzioni II*

6. Sticks of plasticine, laid lightly on the strings or pressed down

    K. Serocki: *Fantasmagoria*
    W. Szalonek: *Mutanza*

7. A pencil, dowel, drumstick, or small piece of wood

    B. Childs: *Nonet*
    G. Crumb: *Night Music I*
    L. Ferrari: *Société II*

8. A coin or small piece of metal

    B. Childs: *Jack's New Bag*

[4]The "Lutheal" piano in Maurice Ravel's *L'Enfant et les sortilèges* is an ordinary piano with a thin strip of paper woven through the strings to dampen their normal resonance.

9. A common artgum eraser

   B. Childs: *Music for Singer*

10. A tambourine

    G. Crumb: *Echoes of Time and the River*

11. A heavy hardbound book

    T. Antoniou: *Lyrics*
    D. Cope: *Parallax*

12. A 7″–8″ pocket comb

    D. Cope: *Parallax*

13. Four milk bottles, side by side, about an inch apart

    D. Bedford: *Piano Piece 2*

In his orchestral work *The Jerusalem Chagall Windows*, Jacob Gilboa directs the pianist to prepare the strings of the lowest section by covering them with a number of antique cymbals; later he places a single large cymbal on the strings, and also several small pieces of metal—presumably bolts or screws. Szalonek in *Proporzioni II* requires a metal rod (triangle beater) to be laid across the strings, as well as wood slabs and iron chains, requirements partially duplicated in Chou Wen-chung's *Cursive* for flute and piano. And in Werner Heider's *-einander*, the piano strings are to be fitted with several rulers (or strips made of plastic or celluloid); when the keys are struck, a clashing (though muted) sound is produced. The same device is also required by Roger Reynolds in his *Mosaic*.

Other players in an ensemble are sometimes directed to "prepare" the piano strings while the pianist is playing at the keyboard. In *Music for Napoleon and Beethoven*, Schwartz asks the trumpet soloist to alternate playing improvisatory sections on his instrument with preparing the piano strings. He stands in the curve of the piano to play and, during moments of rest, inserts between certain strings a number of objects previously placed in a container inside the piano.

Strings

Several curious stringed instrument muting effects have recently been devised by orchestrators of experimental music; these are as follows:

1. The left-hand fingers press the strings down to the fingerboard, deadening the normal resonance, whether played arco or *col legno,* as in:

   E. Brown: *String Quartet*
   L. Hiller: *String Quartet No. 5*
   F. Miroglio: *Réfractions*
   K. M. Nazar: *Variazioni concertanti*

A "skittering" effect is requested by Michael Colgrass in *As Quiet As*, produced by deadening the strings as just described and bouncing the bow, *col legno battuto*, from high on the fingerboard to the bridge.

2. The strings, muffled by grasping them with the left-hand fingers, are played upon either arco or *col legno* (specified in Don Wilson's *Doubles*). A very similar effect is called for in the *Requiem* of Ligeti: the doublebass player is to squeeze a specified string tightly between his left thumb and forefinger while bowing normally. The composer cryptically terms this a "Langlois effect."

3. A doublebass mute is placed on cello strings between the bridge and the end of the fingerboard; the player bows on either side of the mute—that is to say, on either the upper or the lower part of the string (a requirement in the first string quartet of Michael von Biel).

Spatial Muting

Distance can also soften and muffle normal instrumental tone, an acoustical fact that many composers have applied to their sonic requirements. All instruments, singly or collectively, can be stationed off-stage or in remote parts of the auditorium to provide distant ("lontano") effects. Although the basic timbre of an instrument is not drastically altered by remote placement, it is attenuated and softened to a considerable degree. Thus offstage positioning of instruments produces a different, but entirely viable, kind of muting.[5]

Twentieth-century works that have called for this procedure include the following, categorized by orchestral section:

Woodwinds

D. Burge: *Sources III* (clarinet)
G. Crumb: *Echoes of Time and the River* (flutes; clarinets)

---

[5]Henry Brant's article in *Contemporary Composers on Contemporary Music* (Bibliography, page 232) on aspects of spatial composition is especially informative.

M. Gould: *Family Album* (clarinet)

P. Graener: *Flute of Sanssouci* (flute)

Brasses

G. Crumb: *Echoes of Time and the River* (horns; trumpets; trombones)

M. Gould: *Family Album* (horn; trumpet; trombone)

P. Hindemith: *When lilacs last in the door-yard bloom'd* (Army bugle)

C. Ives: *The Unanswered Question* (trumpet)

J. Serebrier: *Momento Psicologica* (trumpet)

P. Standford: *Notte* (horns)

Percussion

G. Crumb: *Echoes of Time and the River* (crotales; glockenspiel plates; suspended cymbals; tam-tams)

Plucked instruments

G. Crumb: *Echoes of Time and the River* (mandolin)

G. Crumb: *Night of the Four Moons* (banjo)

Strings

H. Brant: *Voyage Four* (all strings)

P. Hindemith: *Symphonia Serena* (solo violin; solo viola)

It is tempting to speculate on further novel—as yet undiscovered—methods of muting the various instruments. Whatever may be brought to light, we may be sure that experimental composers will do their part in exploiting the new devices.

3

GLISSANDI

Woodwinds and Brasses

As glissando techniques in woodwind and brass instrument scoring have been fairly common since Mahler's time, they cannot qualify as indubitably "new" devices; their use, however, has become so prevalent in contemporary orchestration and their variants so extensive that special mention must be accorded this particular instrumental technique.

Glissandi are normally achieved on wind instruments through the tightening or relaxing of the embouchure, generally specified by composers and performers as "lip glissandi." Among many works relying on this effect one might cite:

R. L. Finney: *Divertissement*
S. Hodkinson: *Fresco*
D. Martino: *Strata*
D. Reck: *Blues and Screamer; Five Studies for Tuba Alone*

By rolling the mouthpiece into the upper lip, flutists can somewhat extend the range of lip glissandi ("bends"), a directive specified in George Rochberg's *Apocalyptica* and Chou Wen-chung's *Cursive*, for example. Also, by removing the head-joint and inserting a finger in the tubing, then slowly removing it while blowing, one can get an extended glissando from g$\sharp^2$ down to b^1. This version of glissando was required by Boguslaw Schäffer in his *Scultura*.

It is quite common for brass players to create a glissando over the harmonic series of a given fundamental, analogous to the string player's glissando on natural harmonics—the latter a favorite instrumentational device of Ravel and Stravinsky. A few recently published scores that call for the brass version of harmonic glissandi include:

J. Bark, F. Rabe: *Bolos*
J. Druckman: *Animus 1*
K. Huber: *Alveare vernat*
K. Kroeger: *Toccata for Clarinet, Trombone and Percussion*
G. Rochberg: *Tableaux*

Another fairly common and characteristic brass technique is the half-valve glissando on horn, trumpet, or tuba, achieved by pushing down the required valves only half-way while blowing:

M. Ellis: *Mutations* (Example 6)
G. Schuller: *American Triptych*
E. Schwartz: *Music for Napoleon and Beethoven; Rip,* and other works

In David Reck's *Five Studies for Tuba Alone* the composer calls for the player to produce a "bellowing" lip glissando. Other variants of the technique, resulting from combined lip, fingering or slide manipulation, are those staples of jazz performance—"rips," "smears," "squeals," "whinnies," and the like.[1] No longer, of course, are these techniques the exclusive province of jazz and popular expression; they are frequently incorporated into symphonic and chamber scores, even by some composers basically antipathetic to the more commercial forms of contemporary music:

B. Childs: *Jack's New Bag; Nonet,* and other works
M. Ellis: *Mutations* (Example 6)
D. Erb: *Symphony of Overtures*
A. Jolivet: *Suite Transocéane*
G. Rochberg: *Tableaux*

---

[1] Chapter 24 of this writer's *Music Notation—A Manual of Modern Practice* includes a more detailed discussion of various jazz instrumental techniques.

Example 6   Merrill Ellis: from *Mutations* (p. 7)

G. Schuller: *Journey into Jazz; Seven Studies on Themes of Paul Klee*
E. Schwartz: *Music for Napoleon and Beethoven*
K. Stockhausen: *Adieu*

Percussion

Conventional glissandi on timpani, first exploited by Béla Bartók, and glissandi on the pitched mallet instruments are too familiar to contemporary orchestrators to require further explication. Less conventional, and surprisingly effective, is the one-plate glissando available on glockenspiel or vibraphone. To achieve this effect the player with his left hand holds a hard-tipped mallet against the plate to be struck, lightly touching the metal about a half-inch from its end. When the plate is struck with a mallet in the player's other hand, the left-hand mallet is slowly moved to the very end of the metal bar. The aural result is a half-step bending of the pitch, always at a fairly low level of amplitude, it must be stressed. This device is used prominently in Crumb's *Echoes of Time and the River* and in Rochberg's *Tableaux*. For obvious reasons the technique cannot be transferred to the wooden bars of marimba or xylophone.

A simulation of pitch "bend" can, surprisingly, be obtained on a clashed pair of cymbals or crotales; after being struck together the two plates are rapidly shaken in the air, resulting in a perceptible oscillation of frequency (as in the Crumb work just cited).

Qualifying perhaps more as a percussive noise-effect than as a genuine glissando variant is a rapid sweep with a hard mallet or wood stick over the resonators (metal tubes) of vibraphone and marimba; this stipulation appears in:

L. Austin: *The Maze* (Example 7)
F. Miroglio: *Réfractions*
W. Russell: *Fugue for Eight Percussion Instruments*
K. Serocki: *Continuum; Segmenti,* and other works

A point of notational interest is the comparison between Austin's symbology (Example 7) for a resonator glissando and that favored by Serocki in the scores listed:

Example 7   Larry Austin: from *The Maze* (p. 21)

Whereas idiophone glissandi with differently headed mallets are extremely common in modern scores, less prevalent are glissandi with the backs of the fingernails across the metal plates of glockenspiel and vibraphone (as requested in Reginald Smith Brindle's *Orion M.42*, for example). A number of vanguardists have designated that the entire range of the various idiophones be rubbed in ascending or descending spiral patterns with precisely specified stick types— wood, metal, or plastic mallets, wirebrushes, and so on:

L. Foss: *Fragments of Archilochos*
R. Reynolds: *Quick are the Mouths of Earth*
K. Serocki: *Continuum* (Example 8); *Segmenti,* and other works

Simultaneous "black-key" and "white-key" glissandi are by now clichés of contemporary percussion scoring, and their primary interest is notational rather than technical (see Example 8). In parallel or in contrary direction, such chromatic glissandi are prominently displayed in the following recent scores:

T. Baird: *Exhortation*
J. Barraqué: *Chant après chant*
L. Berio: *Circles*
E. Brown: *Available Forms 1*
G. Crumb: *Echoes of Time and the River; Night Music I*
L. Foss: *Fragments of Archilochos*
J. Gilboa: *The Jerusalem Chagall Windows*
A. Jolivet: *Piano Concerto*
M. Kagel: *Anagrama*
F. Miroglio: *Réfractions*
A. Paccagnini: *Musica da Camera*
B. Rands: *Actions for six*
R. Reynolds: *Quick are the Mouths of Earth; Wedge*
K. Serocki: *Fantasmagoria; Segmenti*
K. Stockhausen: *Kontakte; Zyklus*

Example 8   Kazimierz Serocki: from *Continuum* (p. 9)

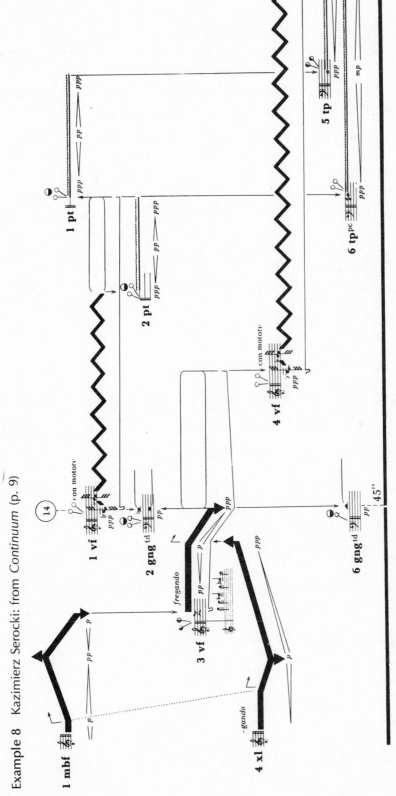

Though it cannot be considered a glissando in the ordinary sense of the term, Kagel's directive in *Sonant* to glissando on the snares of a snare drum deserves mention. The effect is achieved by sliding the stick across the taut snares, the drum turned upside down.

Harp and Other Plucked Instruments

Normally, harp glissandi are played with the fingers of either hand, but one of the earliest experiments of Carlos Salzedo was to slide on the strings with the fingernails—an effect he picturesquely termed "falling hail." As with many of Salzedo's inventions, this device appears frequently in today's scores, including:

L. Berio: *Chemins II; Sequenza II,* and other works
M. Kagel: *Sonant*
M. Kelemen: *Changeant*
P. Méfano: *Paraboles*
B. Rands: *Wildtrack 1*
G. Read: *Haiku Seasons*
C. Salzedo: *Sonata for Harp*
G. Schuller: *Spectra*
E. Varèse: *Offrandes*
Z. Wiszniewski: *Tre pezzi della tradizione*

Played close to the soundboard, the nail glissando becomes a "xyloflux" in Salzedo's terminology. Parenthetically, one might mention that he terms an ordinary glissando a "flux"; played close to the soundboard, it is an "oboic flux." Recent scores that contain this latter technique include:

H. Gorecki: *Monologhi*
P. Méfano: *Paraboles*
G. Read: *Sonoric Fantasia No. 3*
C. Salzedo: various solo harp works

In addition to fingernail glissandi, the strings of the instrument may be stroked or rubbed with the following:

1. The flat fingers
   H. W. Henze: *Being Beauteous*
   B. Rands: *Formants I*

G. Read: *Haiku Seasons*
K. Serocki: *Niobe; Segmenti*

2. The fingernails

S. Matsushita: *Fresque sonore*

3. The palm or flat hand (cluster effect)

G. Becker: *Moirologhi*
L. Berio: *Sequenza II* (Example 4-g)
S. Bussotti: *Fragmentations*
H. Gorecki: *Monologhi*
R. Haubenstock-Ramati: *Petite musique de nuit; Séquences*, and other works
M. D. Levy: *Kyros*
S. Matsushita: *Fresque sonore*
K. Penderecki: *Dimensions of Time and Silence*
B. Rands: *Actions for six*
G. Read: *Haiku Seasons*
Z. Wiszniewski: *Tre pezzi della tradizione*

Salzedo called rubbing with the fingers an "Aeolian tremolo" and with the palm pressing against the strings an "Aeolian rustling." Related to this last technique is the "rolling surf" effect in which a glissando, at a slow tempo, is played with all the fingers bunched together, the normally unused little finger included. In addition to appearing in Salzedo's own works, the device has been requisitioned by Rands in his *Formants I* and by Serocki in *Niobe*.

More conventional variants are simultaneous upward and downward glissandi, usually encompassing the entire instrument range; as precise beginning and ending pitches are not important, composers usually content themselves with writing stems attached to arrow heads below and above the two staves. See, for instance:

K. Serocki: *Segmenti; Symphonic Frescoes*
C. Surinach: *Feria Magica; Melorhythmic Melodramas*
P. Turok: *Chartres West*

Also frequently used in avant-garde scores are Salzedo's "gushing chords," which are very rapid and short-range bursts of glissandi:

S. Barber: *Souvenirs*
L. Berio: *Sequenza II* (Example 4-h)
J. Serebrier: *Colores Magicos*
C. Surinach: *Feria Magica; Melorhythmic Melodramas*

"Gushing chords" can also be played with the thumb fingernail, an action for which Salzedo devised the following notation:

More esoteric glissandi techniques include the following actions:

1. Rapid vertical gliding up on several adjacent wire bass strings with the flat hand ("whistling sounds" in the Salzedo harp manual)

   L. Berio: *Chemins I; Sequenza II*
   S. Bussotti: *Fragmentations; Memoria,* and other works
   E. Denisov: *Romantische Musik*
   D. Erb: *Symphony of Overtures*
   R. Felciano: *Background Music*
   A. Ginastera: *Bomarzo Cantata*
   B. Jolas: *Tranche*
   M. Kagel: *Anagrama; Sonant*
   B. Rands: *Actions for six*
   G. Read: *Sonoric Fantasia No. 3* (Example 25); *Villon*
   T. Takemitsu: *Eucalypts (I)*

2. Vertical sliding on the string(s) with the fingernail(s), either up from the sound-board to as high as the tuning pins, or the reverse, usually on the low wire strings

   M. Kagel: *Sonant* (Example 9-h)

3. Same action, with a mallet or stick

   D. Erb: *The Seventh Trumpet*
   M. Kagel: *Sonant* (Example 9-m)

4. Same action, with a nail file

   R. Felciano: *Background Music*

5. Same action, with the metal end of the tuning key (Salzedo's "fluidic glissando"), and notated as shown below

L. Berio: *Chamber Music*

E. Brown: *Times Five*

S. Bussotti: *Fragmentations*

P. M. Davies: *Revelation and Fall*

J. Druckman: *Windows*

D. Erb: *Concerto for Solo Percussionist; The Seventh Trumpet*

L. Foss: *Orpheus*

H. Holliger: *Glühende Rätsel*

M. Kagel: *Sonant* (Example 9-g)

M. Kelemen: *Changeant*

F. Miroglio: *Réseaux*

G. Read: *Haiku Seasons*

A metal string may also be scraped vertically with the back of a fingernail. In Crumb's *Ancient Voices of Children* the harpist is directed to make a single stroke along the string, lightly and rapidly, creating a nasal and whistling sound which is immediately to be muffled by touching the string with the other hand.

In addition to the glissandi variants just described, the harp strings may be rubbed or stroked horizontally with the following objects:

1. A metal (wire) brush

   H. W. Henze: *Heliogabalus Imperator; Sinfonia N. 6* (Example 39)

   M. Kagel: *Sonant* (Example 9-b, d)

   K. Penderecki: *Anaklasis; The Devils of Loudun*

   K. Serocki: *Niobe*

2. An ordinary hairbrush

   T. Baird: *Espressioni varianti*

   H. Gorecki: *Scontri*

   H. W. Henze: *Heliogabalus Imperator; Sinfonia N. 6*

3. A wooden stick, pencil, or metal rod

   T. Baird: *Espressioni varianti; Exhortation*

   D. Banks: *Tirade*

   B. Bartók: *Concerto for Orchestra*

   G. Crumb: *Ancient Voices of Children*

4. A small board

   H. Gorecki: *Scontri*

5. A plectrum or piece of hard cardboard

   P. M. Davies: *Revelation and Fall*
   H. Holliger: *Siebengesang*

6. A soft rubber plectrum

   R. Moeves: *Et Occidentum Illustra*

Finally, there is Salzedo's "thunder effect"—a rapid and violent glissando limited to the lowest range of the harp, the wire strings being allowed to clash together:

L. Berio: *Chemins I; Sequenza II,* and other works
S. Bussotti: *Mit einem gewissen sprechenden Ausdruck*
R. Felciano: *Background Music*
S. Hodkinson: *Fresco*
M. Kagel: *Sonant* (Example 9-a)
F. Miroglio: *Réseaux*
B. Rands: *Actions for six; Formants I,* and other works
E. Raxach: *Paraphrase*
G. Read: *Haiku Seasons*

Among the other plucked instruments, George Crumb's "bottle-neck" technique on mandolin and banjo (discussed on page 191) qualies as a quasi-glissando device, as does Sidney Hodkinson's directives to the guitarist in *Fresco* to glissando by means of turning the tuning peg of the string just plucked.

Keyboard Instruments

New glissando effects on the piano involve both the keyboard and the interior strings. Foremost among the several key-glissando procedures is a pitchless sliding over the white keys with the back of the fingernails, designated by:

S. Bussotti: *Couple; Pour Clavier,* and other works
B. Rands: *Espressione IV*
R. Reynolds: *Mosaic; Quick are the Mouths of Earth,* and other works

Example 9   Mauricio Kagel: from *Sonant (Faites votre jeu II)*

The same, with a coin held between the fingers:

    N. Castiglioni: *Consonante; A Solemn Music II*

A visually dramatic variant of a conventional key glissando occurs in Russell Peck's *Suspended Sentence:* a two-hand glissando effected with the arms crossed ends with a cluster as far up and down the keyboard as the crossed arms can reach.

In both performance techniques and resultant sounds, interior glissandi directly on the piano strings are immensely varied. They can be achieved laterally or horizontally; that is, the glissando can be along the length of a single string, from near the pinboard to as far up as the player can reach, or it can sweep across the successive strings within any one of the three or four inside sections of the instrument.

Lateral glissandi can be effectuated with the following:

1. The fingertip(s)

    D. Banks: *Assemblies*
    F. Cerha: *Formation et Solution*
    H. Cowell: *The Banshee,* and other solo piano works
    K. Penderecki: *Strophes*
    K. Serocki: *Niobe*

2. The fingernail

    W. Albright: *Danse Macabre*
    D. Burge: *Aeolian Music*
    S. Bussotti: *Couple*
    D. Cope: *Indices*
    G. Crumb: *Ancient Voices of Children; Echoes of Time and the River*
    A. Lanza: *Plectros I, II,* and other works
    T. Lucas: *Aberrations No. VII*
    K. Penderecki: *Strophes*
    E. Schwartz: *Music for Prince Albert*

3. The flat hand

    F. Miroglio: *Réfractions*

4. A wood stick, end of a mallet, flat piece of wood, pencil, or similar object

    I. Anhalt: *Foci*
    E. Boguslawski: *Apokalypsis*
    Z. Bujarski: *Kinoth*

H. Heiss: *Bewegungspiel*
M. Kagel: *Transición* II
Z. Rudzinski: *Contra Fidem*

5. A metal stick or wirebrush

    J. Cage: *First Construction (in Metal)*
    R. L. Finney: *Divertissement*
    W. Kotonski: *Pour quatre*
    K. Penderecki: *Fluorescences*

6. A metal brush of the type used for brushing animals

    I. Anhalt: *Foci*

7. A plectrum or pick

    G. Crumb: *Makrokosmos—Vol. I*
    R. Gerhard: *Concert for 8*
    A. Lanza: *Plectros I, II*
    R. Reynolds: *Blind Men* (Example 10); *Quick are the Mouths of Earth*

8. A dull knife-blade

    B. Childs: *Music for Singer; Nonet,* and other works

9. A nail file

    W. Albright: *Danse Macabre*

10. A coin held like a banjo or mandolin pick (a quarter is the most convenient to grasp)

    R. Reynolds: *Traces*
    W. Russell: *Fugue for Eight Percussion Instruments*

11. The four open edges of one half of a metal tea container (canister) of medium size

    I. Anhalt: *Foci*

12. A cowbell

    L. Foss: *Ni bruit ni vitesse*

13. The bottom edge of a pop bottle or glass tumbler

    D. Erb: *Concerto for Solo Percussionist; The Seventh Trumpet*
    P. Patterson: *Rebecca*

14. A plastic ruler

    A. Janson: *Canon*
    R. Reynolds: *The Emperor of Ice Cream*

Example 10   Roger Reynolds: from *Blind Men* (p. 1)

15. A lump of rosin

B. Childs: *Jack's New Bag*

Generally speaking, the low, wound bass strings of the piano are best for lateral glissandi, owing to their greater length and resonance. And nearly always the sustaining pedal is used in conjunction with glissandi on the strings, whether lateral or horizontal.

In the first volume of *Makrokosmos* for amplified piano, George Crumb combines an intriguing percussive effect with a lateral glissando over the metal winding of a low string. The pianist is directed to "pull plectrum very slowly over string (towards player) while gradually increasing pressure. A series of articulations will be produced by plectrum striking ridges of metal winding."

A curious form of lateral glissando is encountered in Anthony Gilbert's second piano sonata: the composer asks the pianist to strike a designated string centrally with the side of a small bottle or glass tumbler and then slide it toward the far end of the string. And David Bedford in *Come in here child* directs the player to push two milk bottles, one in either hand, up and down certain specified strings, creating a whistling glissando.

Further curiosities: both Stanley Lunetta in his *Piano Music* and Roger Reynolds in *The Emperor of Ice Cream* call for a metal object (triangle beater, large nail, for instance) to be held against a string; after the requisite key is struck, the object is slowly moved along the string, thus altering both timbre and pitch. In his *Proporzioni II* Szalonek requests the same procedure, except that the initial tone is produced by plucking the string rather than striking the key.

All of the objects listed in our discussion of lateral glissandi can be employed in horizontal sweeps across the sectional strings, plus those enumerated below. Today's composers have thus directed their keyboard players to glide, rasp, rub, scrape, stroke, or strum over the strings with the following:

1. The fingertips

   Z. Bujarski: *Kinoth*

   D. Burge: *Aeolian Music*

   G. Crumb: *Echoes of Time and the River; Eleven Echoes of Autumn* (Example 30), and other works

   J. Gilboa: *The Jerusalem Chagall Windows*

   W. Hellermann: *Formata*

   H. Lazarof: *Textures*

   J. Mills-Cockell: *Fragments*

   R. Reynolds: *Blind Men; Wedge,* and other works

   W. Russell: *Fugue for Eight Percussion Instruments*

   E. Schwartz: *Music for Prince Albert; Texture,* and other works

   A. de la Vega: *Exospheres for Oboe and Piano*

   L. Widdoes: *From a Time of Snow*

2. The fingernails

   D. Burge: *Aeolian Music*

   S. Bussotti: *Couple; Il Nudo*

   H. Cowell: *The Banshee,* and other solo piano works

   G. Crumb: *Echoes of Time and the River; Night Music I,* and other works

   L. Ferrari: *Société II*

   L. Foss: *Orpheus*

   A. Gilbert: *Sonata No. 2*

   J. Gilboa: *The Jerusalem Chagall Windows*

   J. M. Horvath: *Die Blinde*

   A. Hrisanide: *Volumes*

   A. Lanza: *Plectros I*

   H. Lazarof: *Textures*

   T. Lucas: *Aberrations No. VII*

   J. Mills-Cockell: *Fragments*

   K. Penderecki: *Strophes*

   R. Reynolds: *Blind Men; Wedge*

W. Russell: *Fugue for Eight Percussion Instruments*
B. Sakač: *Struktur I*
K. Serocki: *Fantasmagoria; Segmenti*
A. de la Vega: *Antinomies for Piano; Structures for Piano and String Quartet*

3. The flat hand

   H. Cowell: *The Banshee*
   L. Ferrari: *Société II*

4. A wirebrush

   W. Albright: *Danse Macabre*
   E. Brown: *Corroboree*
   S. Cervetti: *Six Sequences*
   H. W. Henze: *Sinfonia N. 6*
   S. Hodkinson: *Fresco*
   J. M. Horvath: *Die Blinde*
   A. Hrisanide: *Volumes*
   K. Penderecki: *Anaklasis*
   K. Serocki: *Segmenti*

5. A hairbrush

   Z. Bujarski: *Chamber Piece; Kinoth*
   D. Cope: *Iceberg Meadow*
   H. W. Henze: *Sinfonia N. 6*
   J. Kunst: *Ijzer*
   G. Ligeti: *Atmospheres*
   A. Mellnäs: *Aura*
   W. Szalonek: *Mutanza*

6. A toothbrush

   N. T. Dao: *Tây Nguyên*

7. A gong beater or soft lamb's wool mallet

   J. Cage: *First Construction (in Metal); Imaginary Landscape No. 1*
   J. Kunst: *Ijzer*

8. A piece of cloth, such as a wadded-up handkerchief

   G. Ligeti: *Apparitions*

9. A wood stick or pencil

   D. Cope: *Iceberg Meadow*
   W. Eisma: *Affairs II*
   J. Gilboa: *The Jerusalem Chagall Windows*

H. Heiss: *Bewegungspiel*
M. Kagel: *Transición II*
P. Olsen: *Images*
K. Penderecki: *Anaklasis*
E. Schwartz: *Soliloquies*

10. The point of a lead pencil

    L. Widdoes: *From a Time of Snow*

11. A metal stick or triangle rod

    F. Miroglio: *Réfractions*
    K. Penderecki: *Fluorescences; Sonata per Violoncello e Orchestra,* and other works

12. A steel rod held horizontally

    F. Miroglio: *Réfractions*
    W. Szalonek: *Mutanza*

13. A finger cymbal or crotale

    B. Schäffer: *S'Alto*

14. A cowbell

    L. Foss: *Orpheus*

15. A plectrum or guitar pick

    R. L. Finney: *Divertissement*
    H. Hartwell: *Soul Piece*
    R. Reynolds: *Blind Men* (Example 10); *The Emperor of Ice Cream*

16. A coin, held like a pick

    W. Russell: *Fugue for Eight Percussion Instruments*

17. A comb, of plastic or rubber

    J. Gilboa: *The Jerusalem Chagall Windows*
    P. Patterson: *Rebecca*
    R. Reynolds: *Traces*

18. A knife blade, across the short portions of the strings between the tuning pins and front support

    I. Anhalt: *Foci*

19. The bottom of a straight tumbler, water glass, or a glass ashtray

    W. Albright: *Danse Macabre*
    M. Mitrea-Celarianu: *Seth*

No doubt there are other and equally exotic agents that can be—and have been—used in creating horizontal glissandi on the piano strings. As our vanguard composers continue their search for novel instrumental sounds, other means will be discovered to complement those already in current use.

Accordion

As the modern concert accordion is also a keyboard instrument, albeit a miniaturized version, its players can produce conventional glissandi on its limited bank of white and black keys, normally with the flat fingers or the palm. In his *Piece for Mo* David Bedford directs the accordionist to rub his knuckles up and down the keyboard, creating a rapid and continual "whoosh." Slight pitch bends can also be produced by partially depressing either the keys or the buttons, using maximum bellows pressure.

On the chromatic free-bass accordion, of course, one may glissando as well on the left-hand button keyboard. Each of the three rows of buttons outlines a diminished-seventh chord, progressively pitched a semitone higher, so that a glissando with the flat fingers on any one of the parallel rows would produce that harmonic structure. Although a rapid glissando can be effectuated on any one of the three rows of buttons, because of the necessarily awkward position of the left hand only a very slow slide with the palm can be made on all three rows simultaneously.

The pitchless key-glissando described on page 40 can also be utilized on the remaining standard keyboard instruments—harpsichord, celesta, and organ (the latter minus all registration). Only the various kinds of interior glissandi are limited to the piano, although the more delicate variants might possibly be transferred to the harpsichord interior.

Strings

The symphonies of Gustav Mahler notwithstanding, glissando on the string instruments did not come into its own until Bartók made the device a primary aspect of his string writing (as in the last four string quartets among other works). Today the experimental composer has enlarged both his concept and his usage of string glissando to include the following refinements:

1. Glissando over the string(s) with a very light finger pressure *(glissando effleuré)*, almost as though harmonics were to be produced

    T. de Leeuw: *Spatial Music III*

2. Glissando along the entire length of a string with the bow

    M. Kagel: *Sonant*
    M. Kelemen: *Changeant*

3. Same, with the flat hand

    S. Bussotti: *Mit einem gewissen sprechenden Ausdruck*
    W. Rudzinski: *Pictures from the Holy-Cross Mountains*
    B. Schäffer: *String Quartet*

4. Same, with the fingernail

    D. Bedford: *Five for String Quintet; That White and Radiant Legend*

5. Same, with the edge of a coin or other small metal object

    E. Raxach: *Paraphrase*

6. Same, with a small cymbal (crotale)

    K. Penderecki: *Fluorescences*

7. Same, with a cloth (handkerchief)

    T. Ichiyanagi: *Duet for Piano and String Instrument*

8. Glissando *col legno*, the bow drawn *across* the strings as the left-hand finger slides up or down

    I. Xenakis: *Syrmos*

9. Same, the bow gliding softly *along* the string

    A. Woodbury: *Remembrances*

10. Pizzicato glissando, the sound continued arco glissando, the player overlapping the two sounds as smoothly as possible

    W. Albright: *Danse Macabre*

11. Glissando in two directions simultaneously (possible only on doublebass); achieved by using the thumb on the lower and the 3rd finger on the upper of a pair of adjacent strings

    P. Phillips: *Sonata for String Bass*

12. Glissando (arco or pizzicato) by means of turning the tuning peg with the left hand while bowing or plucking with the right hand. On cello and doublebass it is usually the lowest string that is so treated, the player lowering its pitch as far as possible. Obviously, a tuning-peg glissando can only be downward in pitch direction; a string may be relaxed to the point of total slackness but cannot, on the contrary, be drastically tightened without the danger of snapping. See:

Example 11   Krzysztof Penderecki: from *Fluorescences* (p. 33)

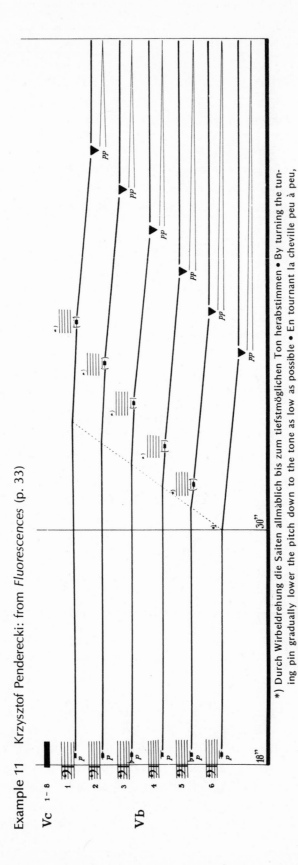

*) Durch Wirbeldrehung die Saiten allmählich bis zum tiefstmöglichen Ton herabstimmen • By turning the tuning pin gradually lower the pitch down to the tone as low as possible • En tournant la cheville peu à peu, relâcher les cordes jusqu'au son le plus bas possible.

L. Berio: *Chemins II*
L. Foss: *Orpheus*
H. Gorecki: *Elementi; Monodram*
G. Ligeti: *Apparitions*
A. Mellnäs: *Aura; Gestes sonores*
P. Norgård: *Prism*
P. Patterson: *Rebecca*
K. Penderecki: *Emanationen; Fluorescences* (Example 11), and other works
R. Reynolds: *Quick are the Mouths of Earth*
B. Schäffer: *Scultura; Violin Concerto,* and other works
I. Xenakis: *ST/4-1, 080262* (Example 3)
Y. Yannay: *preFIX-FIX-sufFIX*

Not an authentic glissando in harmonics but a repeated series of broken, gliding tones is the fancifully termed "seagull harmonic glissando," found in George Heussenstamm's *Pentalogue.* To produce this effect (on doublebass) the left-hand fingers are set in position for an artificial harmonic, the hand then sliding up and down the string, not varying the finger position, while the right hand bows normally.

If further variants of conventional glissandi on all instruments capable of their production are forthcoming in the remaining years of the twentieth century, we may be sure that the experimental composer of the times will exploit the effects to their maximum in his new scores.

4

HARMONICS

Woodwinds

By far the most common use of wind instrument overblowing is to produce harmonics on members of the flute and oboe families. Formerly, harmonics were overblown only at the twelfth from the fingered fundamental (as is required, for instance, in Ravel's *Daphnis et Chloé* and Stravinsky's *Le Sacre du Printemps*). More recently, flute harmonics have been available at the octave (from b^1 up to f^2; those at the twelfth begin with f♯^{2}). Even more recently, certain flutists have devised ways of producing "artificial" harmonics, beginning with d♯^{1} and extending to b^1, when overblowing at the octave takes over.[1]

Octave partials on the flute often result in the harmonic sounding with its fundamental (termed a residual tone); they are produced by enclosing the blowhole tightly with rather loose lips and blowing with strong pressure. See, for example:

G. Ligeti: *Aventures*
W. Szalonek: *Aarhus Music; Les Sons*

[1] See the several articles by John Heiss, listed in the Bibliography.

The general effect of all harmonics on wind instruments is a weaker tone and a reduced amplitude.

For the closely related technique of "whistle (or whisper) tones" on piccolo, flute, and alto flute—very high and clear, but soft, pitches—the air column is directed over the mouthpiece without lip pressure. Actually, "whistle tones" are part of the harmonic series, being the fifth to tenth partials of the overblown fundamental; they have been used in the following works:

P. Chihara: *Willow, Willow*
J. Fortner: *S pr ING*
B. Levy: *Orbs with Flute*
R. Reynolds: *Quick are the Mouths of Earth*

Octave harmonics on oboe are produced by overblowing the fundamental (from b to d♯[1]) and adding the octave key. Above d♯[1] more complicated fingerings and octave key additions are required.[2] Among recent scores requiring the use of oboe and/or English horn harmonics may be mentioned:

G. Amy: *Jeux*
T. Antoniou: *Five Likes*
S. Barber: *Souvenirs*
H. Holliger: *Mobile; Siebengesang*
K. Penderecki: *Capriccio per Oboe*
R. Reynolds: *Quick are the Mouths of Earth*

Certain double harmonics are also possible on the flute and oboe, and several composers have called for trills on these structures; both techniques are illustrated in:

G. Amy: *Jeux*
L. Berio: *Sequenza I; VII*
N. Castiglioni: *Alef*
V. Globokar: *Discours III*
H. Holliger: *Siebengesang*
T. de Kruyf: *Mosaico*
B. Levy: *Orbs with Flute*
K. Penderecki: *Capriccio per Oboe*

[2]Refer to Bruno Bartolozzi's *New Sounds for Woodwind* for fingering charts.

Normally, harmonics are not available to the clarinet or bassoon, but in his *Concerto for Wind Quintet* Donald Martino asks the clarinetist to produce artificial harmonics by closing all the finger holes and muffling the instrument bell against his calf while overblowing the required fundamental of the harmonic. Hans Werner Henze also calls for clarinet harmonics in his orchestral *Heliogabalus Imperator,* but does not instruct the player as to their technical execution or tonal effect.

Percussion

Harmonics are a technical device that would seem logically to be restricted to those instruments of a primarily harmonic and/or melodic nature; one would not ordinarily assume them to be feasible on, or characteristic of, the percussion instruments. Yet several of the tuned percussions can obtain certain partials from a struck fundamental. On timpani, for instance, octave harmonics are available by striking the head of the drum quite close to the rim:

E. Carter: *Eight Pieces for Four Timpani* (Example 12)
W. Kotonski: *Musica per fiati e timpani*
K. Penderecki: *Dimensions of Time and Silence*
K. Serocki: *Segmenti*

Example 12   Elliott Carter: from *Eight Pieces for Four Timpani* (p. 8)

Both the glockenspiel and vibraphone are capable of producing harmonics. The player places the tip of his left forefinger against the center (node) of the struck plate, using a hard mallet to strike the plate. The resulting sound is the third partial, or a pitch two octaves above the fundamental; see, for example:

G. Crumb: *Madrigals—1*
M. Kagel: *Anagrama*

Harp

There has been no significant change in the technique of producing harp harmonics other than the occasional requisition of harmonics at the twelfth in addition to those at the octave. As on the bowed string instruments, partials at the twelfth require the harpist to locate the node at one-third the string length instead of at the half-way point for octave harmonics. See, among other works, Mauricio Kagel's *Sonant* (Example 9-i).

Harpists today are still physically limited to producing only single harmonics with the right hand; double, triple, and even quadruple harmonics are possible with the left hand as long as the pitches created are on contiguous strings (demonstrated in Kagel's work).

Keyboard Instruments

In contemporary piano writing, octave harmonics are extremely common. They are produced by silently depressing the key, or keys, and then sharply striking the key(s) an octave higher or lower than the depressed fundamental(s). Less common, however, are other partials possible—at the twelfth, the fifteenth, and the seventeenth; they are created by touching the proper node on the interior string with the fingertip of one hand while striking the corresponding key with the other hand. Some players facilitate their finding of the requisite node by marking the string with chalk or tape. Among the many recent works exploiting these harmonics are:

S. Bussotti: *Il Nudo; Memoria,* and other works
G. Cacioppo: *Time on Time in Miracles*
N. Castiglioni: *Sequenze*
F. Cerha: *Formation et Solution*
B. Childs: *Jack's New Bag; Music for Trombone*

D. Cope: *Parallax*

G. Crumb: *Ancient Voices of Children; Eleven Echoes of Autumn* (Example 30), and other
  works

R. L. Finney: *Divertissement*

A. Gilbert: *Sonata No. 2*

M. Kagel: *Anagrama*

A. Lanza: *Plectros I, II,* and other works

R. Reynolds: *The Emperor of Ice Cream*

G. Rochberg: *Contra Mortem et Tempus*

J. Spiegelman: *Morsels*

K. Stockhausen: *Klavierstück VI*

It is possible to delay the sounding of a harmonic produced on an interior string
by first striking the key and then pressing the fingertip lightly on the required
node (as in Reynolds' *Blind Men*).

An unconventional manner of producing piano harmonics is used by
George Crumb in his *Ancient Voices of Children* (Example 13) and *Vox
Balaenae*: termed "chisel piano," the technique requires the player to apply the
smooth edge of a ⅝" chisel to a designated string at the node corresponding to
the notated harmonic. The string is then plucked with the fingernail of the other
hand and the chisel is then moved rapidly and decisively along the string so as to
create a series of harmonic pitches. An identical effect is called for in Cage's
First Construction (in Metal), the pianist sliding a metal rod instead of a chisel
along the string. In the *Eleven Echoes of Autumn,* Crumb instructs the player
to "draw a piece of rather hard rubber very slowly along the indicated strings.
When the correct pressure is exerted, a 7th-partial harmonic emerges."

Strings

As for new stringed-instrument concepts of harmonics, first we point out
one or two current refinements, such as the half-harmonic; to achieve this the
left-hand finger touches the string very lightly, but *not* at a harmonic node.
Another method used to obtain a half-harmonic is to press the left-hand fourth
finger on a harmonic node a little more firmly than usual. Both of these procedures produce a flutey sound, roughly akin to the timbres of *sul tasto* and of a
genuine harmonic; one or the other of these techniques is displayed in:

J. Druckman: *Valentine*

H-J. Hespos: *Passagen*

Example 13   George Crumb: from *Ancient Voices of Children* (p. 6)

J. M. Horvath: *Redundanz 2*
M. Kagel: *Match*
I. Yun: *Images*

Harmonics are normally played with the tip or middle of the bow hair; in Michael Colgrass's *As Quiet As* the composer directs that the harmonics be played at the frog of the bow, which imparts a somewhat rougher quality to the sound than usual. Furthermore, harmonics are not often played *col legno,* but Roberto Gerhard includes such a directive to his doublebass player in *Concerto for 8.* The player extends his left hand in a flat position so that it lightly touches all four strings, sliding it up and down as the wood of the bow is bounced on the strings to produce a random series of harmonics.

On the cello and doublebass it is possible to produce what are called "pulled" harmonics; these are natural harmonics fingered in the customary manner, but the string is at the same time pulled sideways with another left-hand finger near the end of the fingerboard. The aural result of this action is a slight bending of the harmonic pitch. Pulled harmonics have been requested by:

P. Chihara: *Logs*
B. Childs: *Jack's New Bag; Nonet,* and other works
J. Druckman: *Valentine*
M. Kagel: *Sonant*
L. Moss: *Windows*

Parenthetically, it may be added that artificial harmonics, formerly unplayable or inordinately difficult to achieve on the doublebass, are now gradually being utilized in solo and chamber literature for this instrument. Artificial harmonics are produced in the higher positions by using the thumb to stop the string and the stretched second or third finger to lightly touch the requisite node.[3] Among the new works conspicuously requiring doublebass artificial harmonics one might mention:

P. Chihara: *Logs*
G. Crumb: *Madrigals—I, IV*
J. Druckman: *Valentine*
L. Harrison: *Suite for Symphonic Strings*
M. Kagel: *Sonant*

[3]See Bertram Turetzky's articles in *The Composer* and his recent book on the contemporary doublebass (Bibliography, p. 233). Turetzky laments the fact that comparatively few composers have so far utilized doublebass artificial harmonics and even fewer players have mastered the technique of playing them.

In some recent scores doublebass players have been required to produce the string equivalent of a wind instrument "enharmonic trill" (see page 138) on overtone pitches, both natural and artificial. This is accomplished by alternately or successively changing fingerings on a specific and repeated pitch, including the shifting of positions (as in Kagel's *Sonant* and Robert Aitken's *Kebyar*).

A recent phenomenon in the basic concept of string instrument harmonics is the discovery and compositional use of the undertone series (also called "sub-harmonics" and "pedal tones"). These are pitches in direct reversal of those obtained in the overtone series (the first partial, or octave, for instance, is *higher* than the open string in the overtone series and *lower* in the undertone series). Sub-harmonics are created by applying fairly heavy bowing pressure on the open string at one or another of the harmonic nodes, and moving the bow very slowly. They have been used conspicuously in at least two recent experimental scores:

G. Crumb: *Black Angels*
A. Woodbury: *Remembrances*

Finally, it should be mentioned that many composers today call for the "highest harmonic possible" on the individual string instruments. In other words, the specific pitch is not as important as the peculiar and strained timbre of the stratospheric pitches so created (see Henze's *Sinfonia N. 6*, Example 39).

5

PERCUSSIVE DEVICES

Woodwinds and Brasses

Percussive effects on the wind instruments may be classified in two categories: those that are produced by the action of the tongue or the breath stream against reed or mouthpiece, and those produced by action of the fingers, hand, or an extraneous object on the body of the instrument. In the former category are sharp, explosive note attacks, with the player enunciating an exaggerated "t," as well as emphatic tongue clicks (velar sounds). Slap-tongue, a staple in older jazz performance techniques and occasionally used by vanguard composers, belongs to this category; it has been stipulated by:

R. Erickson: *Ricercar á 5*
A. Hrisanide: *Clarinet Sonata*
D. Martino: *Strata*
T. Takemitsu: *Voice*

A prolonged use of slap-tongue is roughly akin to flutter-tonguing; it is achieved by letting the tongue come between the lips rather than keeping it behind the teeth as in normal fluttering.

"Tongue-stops" are additional percussive resources for flutists, produced by covering the embouchure hole with the lips and stopping it quickly with the tongue, combined with forceful breath exhalation. The sound is somewhat like

60

key slaps with the mouthpiece covered; it is also markedly akin to string pizzicato. Composers have sometimes designated the effect as *pizz*.

Brass instrumentalists have been instructed by some composers to "pop" the tongue into the mouthpiece (as in Elliott Schwartz's *Rip*), or to produce a percussive tongue attack by pronouncing "fla" into the mouthpiece:

J. Bark, F. Rabe: *Bolos*
V. Globokar: *Discours II; Etude pour Folklora II*
R. Haubenstock-Ramati: *Credentials*

Among the recent works that call for either velar clicks or percussive tongue attacks by woodwind and brass instruments we might cite:

G. Crumb: *Night of the Four Moons*
J. Druckman: *Animus I*
W. Eisma: *Non-lecture II*
J. Fulkerson: *Patterns III*
V. Globokar: *Discours II*
R. Haubenstock-Ramati: *Credentials*
G. Ligeti: *Apparitions*
B. A. Zimmermann: *Tempus loquendi*

All the wind instruments have been called upon to strike the instrument body in some manner, the exact location being always indicated by the composer. Foremost among these possibilities are key or valve clicks: the player's fingers rattle, slap, strike, or tap the keys of woodwind and the valves of brass instruments in a highly audible manner, either combined with normal tone production or divorced from it.[1] A clear notational distinction should be made between these two approaches. Composers today are generally in agreement that an ×-shaped notehead, either on or off the staff

is appropriate for an unpitched key or valve click, while a small cross over a notehead (or under it)

is best for a click combined with specific tone production.

---

[1]It is generally acknowledged that the first use of key slaps occurred in Edgard Varèse's solo flute piece, *Density 21.5* (1936).

A very few of the innumerable recent works requiring both varieties of key and valve claps are:

W. Albright: *Danse Macabre*

E. Brown: *Available Forms 2; From Here,* and other works

P. Chihara: *Willow, Willow*

M. Davidovsky: *Synchronisms No. 1*

V. Globokar: *Accord*

D. Harris: *Ludus II*

J. Heiss: *Movements for Three Flutes*

S. Hodkinson: *Fresco*

H. Holliger: *Siebengesang*

A. Hrisanide: *A la recherche de la verticale*

M. Kelemen: *Entrances*

A. Mellnäs: *Gestes sonores*

F. Miroglio: *Phases*

K. Penderecki: *Fluorescences*

C. Polin: *The Death of Procris* (Example 1)

D. Reck: *Blues and Screamer*

R. Reynolds: *Ambages; Quick are the Mouths of Earth,* and other works

W. Rudzinski: *Pictures from the Holy-Cross Mountains*

E. Schwartz: *Soliloquies; Texture*

H. Sollberger: *Grand Quartet for Flutes*

W. Szalonek: *Concertino per flauto*

A. de la Vega: *Exospheres for Oboe and Piano*

Key and valve clicks, if long extended in duration, produce the percussive equivalent of trill or tremolo; this particular effect has been requisitioned in the following scores:

D. Bedford: *Music for Albion Moonlight; That White and Radiant Legend*

A. Benvenuti: *Polymérie*

L. Berio: *Sequenza I*

S. Bussotti: *Couple*

F. Cerha: *Enjambments*

P. Chihara: *Branches* (Example 14)

B. Childs: *Nonet*

M. Constant: *Winds*

D. Erb: *Concerto for Solo Trombonist; The Seventh Trumpet,* and other works

F. Evangelisti: *Proporzioni*

L. Ferrari: *Société II*

C. Halffter: *Lineas y puntos*

S. Hodkinson: *Interplay*

M. Kelemen: *Equilibres*

D. Martino: *Strata*

K. M. Nazar: *Variazioni concertanti*

C. Polin: *The Death of Procris* (Example 1)

M. Subotnick: *Lamination I*

W. Sydeman: *Concerto da Camera No. III; Texture Studies*

D. Wilson: *Doubles*

In Elliott Schwartz's *Soliloquies*, a gradual crescendo of the impact of the fingers on the keys of flute is coupled with a corresponding diminuendo of the blown pitches to a total absence of tone. A related, delicate effect on all the

Example 14   Paul Chihara: from *Branches* (p. 6)

woodwind members is achieved by lightly fingering a series of specific pitches but without blowing into the mouthpiece or vibrating the reed (as in de la Vega's *Interpolation*).

Though the trombone lacks valves to clack, the equivalent effect can be obtained by rapidly and audibly flipping the F-attachment lever (required in Vinko Globokar's *Accord* and *Discours II*). One wonders, however, how effective this action is on an instrument whose F-attachment lever is well oiled and hence relatively quiet when operated.

Among the available exterior areas of a woodwind instrument that can be lightly struck with the fingers, knuckles, or flat hand, the most obvious is the flaring bell of oboe, clarinet, bass clarinet, or saxophone. On members of the flute family the mouthpiece or the tube opening, with head-joint removed, offer the most convenient locales for striking (as in Zbigniew Bujarski's *Contraria* and Kazimierz Serocki's *Symphonic Frescoes*). An even more unusual action is requested in *Ring* of Toru Takemitsu: the flutist must knock between the mouthpiece and a joint with a finger ring. Obviously, the knocking must be done gently so that the flute surface is not scratched or dented.

English horn, bassoon, and contrabassoon may be struck ad libitum on their elongated tubings. The resultant sounds in all instances, however, are generally weak and inconclusive; no player is willing to strike his instrument with such force that it may be damaged. Exterior percussive effects on the woodwinds, therefore, must be regarded more as psychological visual gestures than as bona fide percussion.

In addition to the several works just cited, the following scores also contain directives for hand-striking on a woodwind instrument:

D. Bedford: *Gastrula*
B. Childs: *Nonet*
W. Sydeman: *Texture Studies*

With the brass instruments, the most likely place for percussive blows with the hand is the bell, either outside on its rim or on the curved inside area. Certain vanguard composers have requested their brass players to rattle, strike, or tap on the instrument bell with the following agents:

1. The fingers, flat palm, or cupped hand

    D. Bedford: *Gastrula; Trona*
    A. Mellnäs: *Tombola*
    K. Serocki: *Symphonic Frescoes*

2. The fingernails

   R. Aitken: *Kebyar*
   D. Cope: *Spirals*
   D. Erb: *The Seventh Trumpet*
   R. Haubenstock-Ramati: *Credentials*
   A. Mellnäs: *Gestes sonores*

3. A metal mute, coin, finger ring, or mouthpiece

   R. Aitken: *Kebyar*
   J. Bark, F. Rabe: *Bolos*
   L. Berio: *Sequenza V*
   J. Cage: *Solo for Sliding Trombone*
   B. Childs: *Jack's New Bag*
   V. Globokar: *Accord*
   W. Heider: *-einander*
   H-J. Hespos: *Passagen*
   S. Hodkinson: *Fresco*
   E. Schwartz: *Rip*
   M. Stibilj: *Condensation*

4. The wood end of a mallet, a plastic-headed stick, or a hard vibraphone mallet

   L. Austin: *Changes*
   B. Childs: *Music for Trombone*
   R. Erickson: *Ricercar à 5*
   E. Krenek: *Five Pieces for Trombone and Piano*

5. A felt-headed mallet, tapped on the bell rim

   L. Austin: *Changes*

6. A wirebrush

   R. Erickson: *Ricercar à 5*

7. A plastic knitting needle

   B. Childs: *Nonet*

Trombonists can also produce several percussive effects not possible on the other brasses. One of these is to stop the bell quickly with a plunger mute:

   T. Albert: *Sound Frames*
   C. Alsina: *Trio 1967*
   V. Globokar: *Discours II*

Another action is to close the slide abruptly so that a sharp metallic click is heard, as required in Vinko Globokar's *Discours II*. A rather special percussive sound can be obtained by rattling a small stick or a pencil inside the curves of the slide (as requested by Barney Childs in *Jack's New Bag* and *Music for Trombone*). And a unique percussive effect utilizing the instrument bell is to be found in both Ernst Krenek's *Five Pieces* and the *Options I* of Elliott Schwartz: the trombonist gently rolls the bell over the strings of a grand piano (with lid off).

The mouthpiece alone of the various brass instruments can also serve as the locale of percussive attack. In "popping" it, for instance, the player hits the cup with his flat palm, as in:

R. Aitken: *Kebyar*
L. Austin: *Changes*
M. Bamert: *Inkblot*
J. Bark, F. Rabe: *Bolos*
D. Bedford: *Gastrula; Trona*
H. Budd: *III for Double Ensemble*
F. Cerha: *Enjambments; Relazioni fragili*
B. Childs: *Jack's New Bag; Music for Trombone*
M. Constant: *Winds*
R. Erickson: *Ricercar à 5*
J. Fulkerson: *Patterns III*
C. Halffter: *Anillos; Lineas y puntos*
R. Haubenstock-Ramati: *Credentials*
S. Hodkinson: *Fresco*
M. Kelemen: *Changeant*
W. Kotonski: *Pour quatre*
E. Krenek: *Five Pieces for Trombone and Piano*
G. Ligeti: *Apparitions*
A. Mellnäs: *Gestes sonores; Tombola*
L. de Pablo: *Modulos III*
W. Rudzinski: *Pictures from the Holy-Cross Mountains*
E. Schwartz: *Options I*
K. Serocki: *Symphonic Frescoes*
M. Subotnick: *Lamination I*
W. Sydeman: *Texture Studies*

In the Jan Bark–Folke Rabe *Bolos* for four trombones, the composers direct that the mouthpiece be struck with another mouthpiece, a very logical as well as effective agent of attack. A rather special tapping procedure is called for in

Larry Austin's *Changes:* the trombonist places the end of the slide on the floor, holding it down with his foot; he then taps on the mouthpiece while slowly drawing the rest of the instrument upward, the slide being pulled out as he does so. The result is a descending "scale" of percussive pitches.

Finally, one cannot neglect to mention several other intriguing effects possible only on trombone: first, audibly sloshing the water in the slide (requested by Vinko Globokar in *Discours II* and by Mihai Mitrea-Celarianu in *Seth*); second, removing the outer slide from the instrument, covering the open ends with the palm and thumb to create a vacuum, and then pulling the tube rapidly out of the slide to make a sharp "vacuum smack" (most notably requisitioned in *Bolos*). Krenek requests the same sound in his *Five Pieces for Trombone and Piano,* but it is achieved by sharply pulling out the F-attachment slide, a gesture duplicated in Donald Erb's *The Seventh Trumpet.*

Harp and Other Plucked Instruments

Percussive devices for the harp are of two basic varieties: those produced on the strings and those effected by striking the frame of the instrument. Included in the first category are percussive attacks with the fingertips, knuckles, nails, or palm. The first usage of this technique was outlined in Carlos Salzedo's *Modern Study of the Harp:*[2] his "tam-tam sounds" were created by filliping a low string with the left-hand second or third finger (or, as a substitute, striking it with a small ivory stick).

Subsequent percussive innovations on the instrument call for flicking, slapping, striking, or tapping the strings with the following agents:

1. The flat fingers or the palm

   L. Berio: *Chemins I; Sequenza II* (Example 4-g)

   Z. Bujarski: *Chamber Piece*

   S. Bussotti: *Fragmentations; Memoria,* and other works

   H. Gorecki: *Monologhi; Scontri*

   B. Jolas: *Tranche*

   M. Kagel: *Anagrama; Sonant*

   M. Kelemen: *Changeant*

   S. Matsushita: *Fresque sonore*

   F. Miroglio: *Réseaux*

   L. de Pablo: *Radial*

---

[2]See Bibliography, page 233.

K. Penderecki: *Dimensions of Time and Silence*
B. Rands: *Formants I*
G. Read: *Sonoric Fantasia No. 3*
C. Salzedo: *Scintillation,* and other solo harp works
L. Schifrin: *Continuum*
K. Serocki: *Segmenti; Symphonic Frescoes*
T. Takemitsu: *Eucalypts (I)*
I. Yun: *Fluktuationen*

2. The fingernails

S. Bussotti: *Fragmentations*
J. Fortner: *S pr ING*
M. Kagel: *Sonant* (Example 9-o)
B. Rands: *Formants I*
K. Stockhausen: *Kontrapunkte*
T. Takemitsu: *Eucalypts (I)*

3. The knuckles

S. Bussotti: *Mit einem gewissen sprechenden Ausdruck*
C. Polin: *Summer Settings*

4. The two hands

M. Kagel: *Sonant* (Example 9-e)
G. Read: *Sonoric Fantasia No. 3*

Plucking the strings with the fingernails was termed "plectric sounds" by Salzedo; the technique is used in many of his works, including the *Sonata for Harp.* Played close to the soundboard, nail pluckings became "guitaric sounds"; they have been used in:

T. Baird: *Erotyki*
G. Crumb: *Madrigals—III*
M. Kelemen: *Changeant*
B. Rands: *Wildtrack 1*
C. Salzedo: various solo harp works
B. Schäffer: *Scultura*
K. Serocki: *Musica concertante*

In many experimental scores of the last several decades one also finds instructions to play on the harp strings (usually in the lowest octave and a fifth, which comprise the wire strings) with the following extraneous agents:

1. Timpani mallets (soft, medium, hard)

   S. Bussotti: *Fragmentations*
   G. Crumb: *Echoes of Time and the River; Madrigals—IV*
   H. Holliger: *Siebengesang*
   M. Kagel: *Anagrama; Sonant* (Example 9-k)
   S. Matsushita: *Fresque sonore*
   K. Penderecki: *Anaklasis*
   B. Rands: *Actions for six*
   G. Read: *Haiku Seasons*
   Z. Wiszniewski: *Tre pezzi della tradizione*

2. A wooden drumstick or piece of wood

   M. Kagel: *Sonant* (Example 9-l)

3. A hammer or a chime mallet

   Y. Sadai: *Nuances*

4. A metal stick (triangle rod)

   G. Amy: *Trajectoires*
   L. Berio: *Chemins I*
   M. Kagel: *Sonant* (Example 9-s)

5. A rubber-covered metal rod

   H. Holliger: *Siebengesang*

6. The tuning key (metal end)

   D. Erb: *Symphony of Overtures*
   S. Matsushita: *Fresque sonore*
   F. Miroglio: *Réseaux*

7. A plectrum or guitar pick

   G. Crumb: *Echoes of Time and the River*
   H. W. Henze: *Heliogabalus Imperator*
   K. Serocki: *Segmenti*
   W. Szalonek: *Concertino per flauto*
   I. Yun: *Symphonische Szene*

8. Wirebrushes

   G. Arrigo: *Infrarosa*
   M. Kagel: *Sonant* (Example 9-b, f)
   K. Penderecki: *The Devils of Loudun*

9. Two bottle brushes about 1 cm in width

   Borup-Jorgenson: *Nordisk Sommer Pastoral*

10. An antique cymbal (crotale)

    L. Foss: *Elytres*

11. An 18″ ruler

    D. Erb: *Symphony of Overtures*

12. A woman's 9″ comb with half dense and half sparse rows of teeth and an ordinary 5″ pocket comb

    Y. Yannay: *Coloring-Book for the Harpist*

Remarkably similar to a deep gong stroke is the sound of the low wire harp strings when struck with mallets or a hammer. Though not to be compared in resonance with this action, an intriguing direction to rattle a pencil between two wire strings occurs in Don Banks's *Tirade* and in R. Murray Schafer's *Requiems for the Party-Girl.* The resulting sound can be fairly violent or delicately restrained, depending upon the intensity of the rattling.

When the player is seated at his instrument, not many areas of the harp frame are readily accessible for percussive striking. The most obvious locale, and the one most easily reached, is the wide soundboard; predictably, the majority of nonstring percussive effects are created in this area. As with the strings themselves, the soundboard can be drummed upon, struck sharply, or tapped lightly with the following agents:

1. The fingertips

   S. Bussotti: *Fragmentations*
   J. Fortner: *S pr ING*
   M. Kagel: *Anagrama; Sonant*
   F. Miroglio: *Réseaux*
   B. Rands: *Formants I*
   G. Read: *Haiku Seasons*

2. The palm or open hand

   G. Becker: *Moirologhi*
   S. Bussotti: *Fragmentations*
   R. Felciano: *Background Music*
   H. Holliger: *Siebengesang*
   B. Maderna: *Stele per Diotima*
   S. Matsushita: *Fresque sonore*
   B. Rands: *Formants I*

3. The knuckles

> L. Berio: *Chemins I; Circles,* and other works
> S. Bussotti: *Fragmentations*
> D. Erb: *Symphony of Overtures*
> R. Felciano: *Background Music*
> S. Matsushita: *Fresque sonore*
> B. Rands: *Formants I; Wildtrack I*
> G. Read: *Haiku Seasons*

4. The fingernails

> K. Stockhausen: *Kontrapunkte*

5. The tuning key

> Y. Sadai: *Nuances*
> B. Sakač: *Struktur I*

6. A stick or mallet

> S. Bussotti: *Fragmentations*
> M. Kagel: *Sonant* (Example 9-l)
> Y. Sadai: *Nuances*

The back of the soundboard—the rounded part that rests against the player's right shoulder—can be struck with the flat hand (as in Kagel's *Sonant*) or with the knuckles:

> L. Berio: *Sequenza II* (Example 4-f)
> S. Bussotti: *Mit einem gewissen sprechenden Ausdruck*
> G. Crumb: *Ancient Voices of Children; Madrigals—III*

Striking the brass plate above the tuning pins with the end of the tuning key is another Salzedo invention. Termed the "anvil effect," the technique is appropriately identified by the following notational symbol:

Surprisingly, relatively few contemporary instrumentators have availed themselves of this device; among the many works surveyed it showed up only in Bussotti's unique *Fragmentations* and in Sydney Hodkinson's orchestral *Fresco*. A few composers, however, have designated that the metal front column be struck with the tuning key or other metal object. It should be pointed out that most harpists will strongly—and rightly—resist such a directive as being damaging to their instrument. Composers would be well advised, therefore, to restrict any metallic blows on the harp to the curving brass plate at the top of the instrument.

Several closely related effects combine normal plucking of the strings with percussive blows on the soundboard. First—from a chronological standpoint, at least—are Salzedo's "timpanic sounds": the right hand taps the soundboard with the third finger while the left hand plucks the string(s). See various of Salzedo's solo harp pieces, as well as Bussotti's *Fragmentations*, Varèse's *Ameriques*, and *Kyros* of Marvin David Levy. A variant of this technique is to pluck the string at its lower end and beat simultaneously on the soundboard with a finger of the same hand:

G. Becker: *Moirologhi*
V. Globokar: *Voie*
M. Kagel: *Anagrama; Sonant* (Example 9-q)
T. de Kruyf: *Einst den Grau*
B. Maderna: *Stele per Diotima*

In his *Sequenza II* (Example 4-b) Berio directs the harpist to play *près de la table,* letting the finger slide immediately and vigorously to the soundboard after plucking the string. This is also requested in:

E. Brown: *Available Forms 2*
S. Bussotti: *Fragmentations*
M. Kagel: *Sonant*
F. Miroglio: *Réseaux*
B. Rands: *Formants I*
T. Takemitsu: *Eucalypts (I)*

Guitar, Mandolin, and Banjo

In many avant-garde scores the guitar appears more frequently and performs more unconventionally than either the mandolin or banjo. Mainly, the newer guitar effects are percussive in nature and include actions both on the strings and the body. The most common directive in the first category is to slap the strings vigorously against the fingerboard with the left hand; this action has been stipulated by:

A. Bloch: *Dialoghi*
D. Erb: *String Trio*
M. Kagel: *Sonant* ·
W. Kotonski: *a battere*

A guitarist can also simulate "snap" pizzicato by plucking a string so violently that it rebounds against the fingerboard (see Cristobal Halffter's *Codex I* and Bartolozzi's *Concertazioni per Oboe*).

In both his *a battere* and *Concerto per quatro*, Kotonski asks the guitarist to strike a string with a right-hand finger and then press it to the fingerboard. This action sets both segments of the string in vibration and produces a faint double-stop effect combined with a subtle percussive noise. In George Crumb's *Night of the Four Moons*, the banjo player obtains a delicate murmuring by trilling on one string with two thimble-capped fingers.

The strings of all three instruments can be rubbed or stroked with the fingers or flat hand to create a soft percussive coloration (as in Sydney Hodkinson's *Fresco*); or a single string can be deadened with the left hand and then stroked with a fingernail of the right hand (requested in Lukas Foss's *Fragments of Archilochos*).

All three instruments can be struck on their backs, sides, top, or fingerboard with the player's fingers, thumb, knuckles, nails, or palm:

L. Foss: *Fragments of Archilochos; Paradigm*
R. Gerhard: *Concert for 8*
S. Hodkinson: *Fresco*
M. Kagel: *Sonant*
W. Kotonski: *a battere*
G. Read: *Canzone di Notte*

In his *Nuances,* Yizhak Sadai asks the guitarist to strike the back of the instrument while pressing down all the strings. It is also possible (and effective) to strike the bridge of either guitar or mandolin with the hand; see the following works:

G. Arrigo: *Tre Occasioni*
L. Foss: *Fragments of Archilochos*
G. Read: *Canzone di Notte*

Keyboard Instruments

Of the several keyboard instruments available to the contemporary composer, the piano offers the greatest possibility for percussive use. Sounds so produced may originate on various areas of the interior—the strings or the metal frame—or on the exterior body of the instrument.[3] Without a doubt, the most common method of interior playing is to pluck a string, quasi-pizzicato, with the following diverse agents:

1. The fingertip

    W. Albright: *Danse Macabre*
    E. Brown: *Music for Cello and Piano*
    S. Bussotti: *Five Pieces for David Tudor; Il Nudo,* and other works
    G. Crumb: *Eleven Echoes of Autumn*
    A. Lanza: *Plectros I, II*
    H. Lazarof: *Textures*
    I. Lidholm: *Poesis*
    J. Mills-Cockell: *Fragments*
    E. Schwartz: *Music for Prince Albert*
    K. Serocki: *Fantasmagoria*
    J. Spiegelman: *Morsels*
    A. de la Vega: *Antinomies for Piano*

2. Two fingers

    M. Ishi: *Aphorismen*

3. The fingernail

    W. Albright: *Danse Macabre*
    R. du Bois: *Pour faire chanter*
    S. Bussotti: *Couple; Il Nudo,* and other works
    G. Crumb: *Eleven Echoes of Autumn* (Example 30); *Night Music I, II*
    M. Davidovsky: *Inflexions*
    A. Gilbert: *Sonata No. 2*
    R. Haubenstock-Ramati: *Credentials*
    W. Hellermann: *Formata*
    G. Read: *Haiku Seasons*
    E. Schwartz: *Music for Prince Albert*
    A. de la Vega: *Antinomies for Piano*

[3]It should be readily understood that all of the effects catalogued here are feasible only on a grand piano, usually with the lid and music rack removed.

4. A plectrum or pick (an ordinary paper clip makes a good substitute)

I. Anhalt: *Foci* (Example 15)

E. Brown: *Corroboree*

B. Childs: *Jack's New Bag; Nonet*

P. M. Davies: *Eight Songs for a Mad King*

R. L. Finney: *Divertissement*

M. Ishi: *Aphorismen*

A. Lanza: *Plectros I, II*

A. Mellnäs: *Tombola*

M. Mitrea-Celarianu: *Seth*

L. de Pablo: *Libro para el pianista*

R. Reynolds: *Blind Men; Quick are the Mouths of Earth*

B. Schäffer: *Scultura*

W. Szalonek: *Les Sons*

5. A dinner fork

W. Russell: *Fugue for Eight Percussion Instruments; Three Dance Movements*

Plucking the string close to the pegs imparts a hard, metallic bite to the tone; plucking near the center of the string produces a more mellow quality to the sound. The higher strings have less sustaining power than the lower octaves, and are brittle and thin when plucked.

In addition to the above-described methods of interior pizzicato, the strings of the piano can be patted, slapped, struck, or tapped with a wide selection of agents. Methods that rely on the use of the player's two hands include the following:

1. The fingertips

F. Cerha: *Formation et Solution*

Chou Wen-chung: *Cursive*

G. Crumb: *Makrokosmos—Vol. I; Night Music I*

H. Dianda: *Estructuras*

J. M. Horvath: *Die Blinde*

A. Lanza: *Plectros I, II*

H. Lazarof: *Textures*

K. Penderecki: *Strophes*

J. Spiegelman: *Morsels*

2. The fingernails

S. Bussotti: *Five Pieces for David Tudor; Il Nudo,* and other works

G. Crumb: *Five Pieces for Piano; Night Music I,* and other works

Example 15 Istvan Anhalt: from *Foci* (p. 110)

A. Gilbert: *Sonata No. 2*

R. Reynolds: *Quick are the Mouths of Earth*

A. de la Vega: *Antinomies for Piano*

3. The knuckles

J. Mills-Cockell: *Fragments*

A. de la Vega: *Antinomies for Piano*

4. The palm or open hand

D. Burge: *Aeolian Music*

S. Bussotti: *Il Nudo; Mit einem gewissen sprechenden Ausdruck,* and other works

G. Crumb: *Echoes of Time and the River; Night Music I,* and other works

H. Dianda: *Estructuras*

D. Erb: *The Seventh Trumpet*

L. Ferrari: *Société II*

R. L. Finney: *Divertissement*

J. Gilboa: *The Jerusalem Chagall Windows*

R. Haubenstock-Ramati: *Credentials*

M. Kagel: *Transición II*

W. Kilar: *Dipthongos*

W. Kotonski: *Pour quatre*

A. Lanza: *Plectros I, II,* and other works

I. Lidholm: *Poesis*

T. Lucas: *Aberrations No. VII*

A. Mellnäs: *Tombola*

L. de Pablo: *Reciprico*

R. Reynolds: *Wedge*

E. Schwartz: *Music for Napoleon and Beethoven* (Example 21)

K. Serocki: *Niobe; Symphonic Frescoes,* and other works

W. Szalonek: *Proporzioni II*

A. de la Vega: *Antinomies for Piano; Exospheres for Oboe and Piano*

L. Widdoes: *From a Time of Snow*

R. Wittinger: *Espressioni*

5. The edge of the open hand

B. Rands: *Wildtrack 1*

6. The clenched fist

N. T. Dao: *Tây Nguyên*

A. Lanza: *Plectros I, II*

G. Read: *Haiku Seasons*

A. de la Vega: *Exospheres for Oboe and Piano; Structures for Piano and String Quartet*

Extraneous objects used in playing upon the piano strings, as found in recently published scores, include:

1. Mallets or drumsticks (such as soft timpani, hard rubber, sponge-headed, medium plastic, bamboo, and so on)

    I. Anhalt: *Foci*
    R. du Bois: *Pour faire chanter*
    E. Brown: *Music for Cello and Piano*
    G. Crumb: *Echoes of Time and the River; Night Music I*
    H-U. Engelmann: *Cadenza*
    D. Erb: *Symphony of Overtures*
    J. Gilboa: *The Jerusalem Chagall Windows*
    C. Halffter: *Planto por las victimas de la violencia*
    H. Hartwell: *Soul Piece*
    R. Herder: *Requiem II*
    H. Holliger: *Siebengesang*
    A. Hovhaness: *Jhala,* and other piano works
    A. Lanza: *Plectros I, II*
    H. Lazarof: *Espaces*
    A. Mellnäs: *Tombola*
    K. M. Nazar: *Variazioni concertanti*
    P. Norgård: *Symphony No. 2*
    M. Ohana: *Sorôn-Ngô*
    K. Penderecki: *De Natura Sonoris (I); Dimensions of Time and Silence,* and other works
    H. Pousseur: *Honeyrêves*
    R. Reynolds: *Blind Men; The Emperor of Ice Cream,* and other works
    W. Russell: *Fugue for Eight Percussion Instruments*
    E. Schwartz: *Music for Napoleon and Beethoven*
    A. de la Vega: *Antinomies for Piano*
    R. Wittinger: *Espressioni*

2. Wirebrushes

    I. Anhalt: *Foci* (Example 15)
    G. Crumb: *Night Music II*
    H. W. Henze: *Sinfonia N. 6*
    J. M. Horvath: *Die Blinde*
    A. Janson: *Canon*
    K. M. Nazar: *Variazioni concertanti*
    L. de Pablo: *Libro para el pianista; Modulos III*

K. Penderecki: *Dimensions of Time and Silence*
R. Reynolds: *The Emperor of Ice Cream*

3. Triangle beaters or thin metal rods

L. Foss: *Ni bruit ni vitesse*

4. A steel rod held vertically

W. Szalonek: *Mutanza*

5. Knitting needles

A. Mellnäs: *Tombola*

6. Pencils (with the wood or the metal end)

D. Cope: *Iceberg Meadow*
J. Gilboa: *The Jerusalem Chagall Windows*
G. Heussenstamm: *Seventeen Impressions*
T. Lucas: *Aberrations No. VII*
R. Swift: *Piano Concerto*

7. A clave or piece of wood

M. Finnissy: *As When Upon a Tranced Summer Night*
C. Halffter: *Planto por las victimas de la violencia*

8. Teaspoons

J. Kunst: *Ijzer*
L. Moss: *Omaggio*

9. A metal plate or a cymbal

K. Penderecki: *Fluorescences*
B. Schäffer: *S'Alto*
R. Wittinger: *Concentrazione*

10. An antique cymbal (crotale)

G. Crumb: *Night Music I*

11. A plastic fly swatter or ruler

B. Childs: *Jack's New Bag*
C. Halffter: *Noche Pasiva del Sentido; Planto por las victimas de la violencia*
P. Patterson: *Rebecca*

12. A screwdriver

N. T. Dao: *Tây Nguyên*

13. A hammer

   Y. Sadai: *Nuances*

14. A hairbrush

   E. Bujarski: *Kinoth*
   H. W. Henze: *Sinfonia N. 6*
   J. Kunst: *Ijzer*
   A. Mellnäs: *Tombola*

15. A clothes brush and a toothbrush

   N. T. Dao: *Tây Nguyên*

16. A water glass or small bottle

   M. Mitrea-Celarianu: *Seth*

17. The metal edge of a wooden ruler

   D. Cope: *Parallax*

18. Thimble-capped fingers

   G. Crumb: *Makrokosmos—Vol. I*
   J. M. Horvath: *Die Blinde*
   A. Lanza: *Plectros I, II*

19. The fingers of a leather glove (not worn!)

   G. Ligeti: *Nouvelles Aventures*

Indubitably effective as a percussive device but patently hard on the piano strings is the directive to drop a large piece of wood or a heavy metal bar onto the strings of the lowest section, leaving the sustaining pedal down and allowing the sound to vibrate until it dies away. This effect has been requisitioned in:

   H-U. Engelmann: *Cadenza*
   M. Kagel: *Transición II*
   A. Lanza: *Plectros II*
   K. Penderecki: *Anaklasis; Cantata in Honorem Alma Matris,* and other works
   W. Szalonek: *Mutanza*
   R. Wittinger: *Espressioni*

In Penderecki's *Dies Irae,* and *Grablegung Christi* a similar result is obtained by dropping a hand cymbal onto the strings. And Szalonek in his *Mutanza* also requests that steel balls, 15 to 20 cm in diameter, be poured onto the strings of one section; ordinary marbles could also be used for this action, though the resulting sound might be less sharp and decisive.

In *Ni bruit ni vitesse* (Example 16) Lukas Foss has the pianist play upon the keyboard while an assistant drops a pair of Japanese lacquer bowls on the strings. In the same work, the bowls—gently placed on certain strings—are shoved with the pianist's hand to produce a faint sound, or the piano itself is pushed by the player to reactivate the lingering sound.

There is an amusing 30-second sequence in Paul Patterson's *Rebecca* in which the pianist continuously drops several tennis balls onto the interior strings, the pedal depressed, to the accompaniment of deflating balloons.

Pitchless percussive noises can be produced on the exterior surfaces or various interior parts of the piano. Avant-gardists are usually quite precise in designating areas to be struck in some manner. On the outside of the instrument these include the sides next to the keyboard, under the keyboard, the top surfaces, or the music rack if one is used. These areas may be struck with the flat fingers, palm, fingernails, knuckles, clenched fist, or with a stick or similar object. Such requirements are prominently displayed in:

W. Albright: *Danse Macabre*

D. Banks: *Tirade*

D. Bedford: *Music for Albion Moonlight*

R. du Bois: *Pour faire chanter*

S. Bussotti: *Couple; Five Pieces for David Tudor*

J. Cage: *The Wonderful Widow of Eighteen Springs*

B. Childs: *Jack's New Bag; Music for Trombone,* and other works

G. Crumb: *Echoes of Time* and *the River; Night Music I,* and other works

L. Ferrari: *Société II*

S. Garant: *Cage d'Oiseau*

W. Heider: *Landschaftspartitur*

S. Hodkinson: *Fresco*

M. Ishi: *Aphorismen*

M. Kelemen: *Changeant*

I. Lidholm: *Poesis*

G. Ligeti: *Apparitions*

T. Lucas: *Aberrations No. VII*

B. Maderna: *Stele per Diotima*

J. Mills-Cockell: *Fragments*

P. Olson: *Images*

B. Rands: *Espressione IV*

R. Reynolds: *The Emperor of Ice Cream*

Example 16   Lukas Foss: from *Ni bruit ni vitesse* (p. 10)

60 sec.

Take two Japanese bowls, one in each hand. Alternately, drop one at a time on the strings raised by the dampers of the previous cluster (canon). The dropping of a bowl over the strings must rhythmically coincide exactly with the piano keys cluster. *Repeat in part if there is time left.*

Duration of each cluster totally irregular, as if trying to trip up the percussionist (but do not succeed).

senza pedale

Perc.

Pianist

I

p

B. Schäffer: *Scultura*

E. Schwartz: *Septet; Soliloquies,* and other works

K. Serocki: *Fantasmagoria*

A. de la Vega: *Antinomies for Piano; Exospheres for Oboe and Piano*

Other agents required in recent works have included a coin (denomination unspecified, in Krenek's *Sonata for Flute*); a wood ruler (in *Société II* of Luc Ferrari), and a plastic fly swatter (in Barney Childs's musical catch-all, *Jack's New Bag*).

The piano pedal can also be utilized percussively: it can be sharply depressed so that one hears not only a noise but the added resonance of the strings vibrating; or the foot can strike the pedal forcibly without depressing it fully. These several usages can be seen in the following scores:

D. Bedford: *Music for Albion Moonlight*

M. Finnissy: *As When Upon a Tranced Summer Night*

A. Gilbert: *Sonata No. 2*

M. Kagel: *Transición II*

A. Lanza: *Plectros I, II*

P. Lewis: *Sweets*

F. Miroglio: *Réfractions*

B. Schäffer: *Musica per pianoforte*

In his orchestral *Heterophonie*, Kagel requests a percussive pedal effect on the celesta; no examples for harpsichord pedals have so far been observed.

Much favored by today's avant-gardist, possibly for visual as well as for auditory shock value, is slamming down the keyboard cover:

S. Bussotti: *Couple; Il Nudo,* and other works

J. Cage: *Music of Changes IV*

J. Christou: *Enantiodromia*

S. Hodkinson: *Fresco*

A. Hrisanide: *Volumes*

T. Mayuzumi: *Metamusic*

P. Patterson: *Rebecca*

R. Reynolds: *Wedge*

B. Schäffer: *Musica per pianoforte*

E. Schwartz: *Soliloquies*

R. Wilding-White: *Whatzit No. 1*

Interior piano areas available for percussion use include the metal frame or cross-beams, the tuning pins, the wooden sides, and the soundboard—the latter struck through the largest hole in the metal frame; see the following works for examples of interior percussion:

W. Albright: *Danse Macabre*
D. Burge: *Aeolian Music*
S. Bussotti: *Mit einem gewissen sprechenden Ausdruck*
G. Crumb: *Echoes of Time and the River; Night Music I,* and other works
L. Foss: *Orpheus*
P. Norgård: *Symphony No. 2*

Although, strictly speaking, it is not a percussive effect, mention should be made of Witold Szálonek's directive in *Mutanza* to rub the surface of the soundboard with a nylon cork. Foss includes a parallel direction to the keyboard player in *Orpheus* to rub a wooden chime mallet along the soundboard.

As with the other interior techniques on piano, contemporary composers have generally been careful to designate specific agents of attack on cross-beams, tuning pegs, and related areas:

1. The fingers

   E. Schwartz: *Septet; Soliloquies*

2. The fingernails

   G. Crumb: *Night Music I*

3. The knuckles

   W. Albright: *Danse Macabre* (Example 17)
   D. Burge: *Aeolian Music*
   G. Crumb: *Eleven Echoes of Autumn* (Example 30); *Makrokosmos—Vol. I*
   L. Ferrari: *Société II*
   A. Janson: *Canon*
   E. Schwartz: *Septet; Soliloquies*

4. A stick or mallet

   D. Burge: *Aeolian Music*
   S. Bussotti: *Il Nudo*
   D. Cope: *Parallax*
   G. Crumb: *Night Music I*
   B. Maderna: *Stele per Diotima*

Example 17   William Albright: from *Danse Macabre* (p. 14)

R. Reynolds: *Wedge*

E. Schwartz: *Music for Napoleon and Beethoven* (Example 21)

5. A coin or small metal object

M. Ishi: *Aphorismen*

W. Szalonek: *Proporzioni*

6. A hammer

B. Childs: *Jack's New Bag*

7. The spine of a heavy hardbound book

D. Cope: *Indices*

In his fancifully titled *Mit einem gewissen sprechenden Ausdruck,* Bussotti directs the pianist to draw a metal stick heavily along the tuning pins, an action that produces an impressive clatter.

In addition to the pitchless glissando over the white keys (mentioned on page 40), Roger Reynolds further stipulated in *Blind Men* that the player rasp the wood end of a mallet across the edges of both white and black keys, resulting in a rhythmic clacking. Similarly, in Barney Childs's work cited above the pianist is to glissando along the fronts of the white keys with a wood stick.

Three closely allied percussive key effects have been utilized by Kagel in *Anagrama:* an already depressed key is struck sharply with the finger, making an audible click; a key is struck with a ring on the player's finger; and a key is held by the fingers of one hand (without being depressed) and then struck with a finger ring.

In his various piano works Bussotti invariably requests that the keys be tapped or trilled upon with the fingertips or nails, but so lightly that the keys are not depressed and one hears only faint percussive clickings (as in the *Five Pieces for David Tudor*). These same actions are also requested by Niccolo Castiglioni in *Consonante* and by Kagel in his solo organ *Improvisation ajou-tée*.

The accordion—especially the modern free-bass model—is capable of some unusual percussive effects, although to date few composers for the instrument have notably availed themselves of these particular sound resources. Among the several possibilities one might list: 1) slapping the keys very lightly to create a percussive impact to the pitch(es) sounded; 2) audibly clicking the registration switches, rather akin to the sound of woodwind instrument key clacks; 3) flicking the nail on the bellows snaps; 4) running the finger, or a stick or pencil, along the opened bellows; 5) knocking with the fingers or knuckles on various parts of the instrument; 6) tapping with the palm on the front side of the opened bellows—a sound that is remarkably drumlike and resonant.

Strings

Possibly no avant-garde string technique is more varied in production or more intriguing sonically than the concept—currently high in favor—of the bowed strings as percussion rather than lyric instruments. As with the keyboard instruments, there are basically two modes of producing percussive sounds: the strings themselves are struck in various manners, or the body of the individual instrument becomes the locale for varied attack. Precise areas on the strings or on the instrument frame are indicated and the striking agents are specifically designated by the great majority of composers.

In point of historical development, *col legno* was the earliest percussive technique applied to the bowed string instruments. Although striking the strings with the wood of the bow was first utilized by composers as early as 1605, it was rare even in nineteenth-century string literature.[4] Not until the early part of the present century did the technique become firmly rooted in orchestrational practice; at the same time it assumed an increasingly important role in chamber music for strings (the quartets of Schoenberg, Berg, and Webern, for instance). Today a number of viable variations of the *col legno* technique have appeared in vanguard scores; these may be catalogued as follows:

1. The string is struck or rubbed with the hair and wood of the bow simultaneously, the bow being turned on its side; whether specifically requested or not, this is the manner in which most string players respond to *col legno* directives

   C. Alsina: *Trio 1967*
   K. Gaburo: *Antiphony IV; Two*
   M. Kagel: *Match; Sonant*
   W. Sydeman: *Projections I; Texture Studies*

2. The strings are struck over the fingerboard with the wood of the bow *(col legno battuto)*

   M. Kagel: *Sexteto de cuerdas*

3. The strings are struck directly over the bridge, *col legno*

   M. Davidovsky: *Synchronisms No. 3*
   L. Harrison: *Suite for Symphonic Strings*
   A. Lanza: *Cuarteto V*
   S. Matsushita: *Fresque sonore*
   P. Méfano: *Paraboles*
   S. Wiechowicz: *Lettre à Marc Chagall*

4. The strings are gently stroked or rubbed with the back of the bow *(col legno frotté)*

   W. Rudzinski: *Pictures from the Holy-Cross Mountains*

5. The left-hand fingernail strikes the string at the same time that the back of the bow taps the same string

   M. Kagel: *Match*

---

[4]In Tobias Hume's *Musical Humors,* according to Bertram Turetzky *(The Contemporary Contrabass).* Turetzky's book, incidentally, contains not only a veritable goldmine of information on his instrument but, like Bartolozzi's *New Sounds for Woodwind,* is a pioneer in the whole area of research into contemporary instrumental techniques.

6. *Col legno battuto* is combined simultaneously with left-hand pizzicato on the same string

    S. Cervetti: *Zinctum*

7. The same, combined with glissando on the string

    D. Erb: *Trio for Two*
    M. Kagel: *Sexteto de cuerdas*

8. The strings are deadened with the left-hand fingers or palm, the wood of the bow then bouncing from the fingerboard to the bridge, creating a "skittering" effect

    M. Colgrass: *As Quiet As*
    J. Druckman: *Animus 2; String Quartet No. 2*
    L. Ferrari: *Société II*
    K. M. Nazar: *Variazioni concertanti*

9. With the left-hand fingers in first position (on violin and viola), lightly touching the strings as for harmonics, the bow-wood is bounced freely along the length of a pair of strings; the motion is from on or near the bridge toward the fingers

    M. Powell: *Filigree Setting* (Example 18)

10. Same, on cello (possible also on doublebass); the motion is from the end of the fingerboard to the bridge

    J. Druckman: *Incenters*
    M. Powell: *Filigree Setting*

11. *Col legno battuto* on the strings behind the bridge; according to Lou Harrison, on the doublebass this will produce "a slightly 'pingy' semi-pitched drumming, whose sound will suggest both that of the marimbula and that of certain Oriental drums."

    L. Berio: *Epifanie*
    E. Brown: *String Quartet*
    B. Childs: *Nonet*
    M. Davidovsky: *Synchronisms No. 3*
    R. Gerhard: *Concerto for Orchestra*
    A. Ginastera: *Bomarzo Cantata*
    L. Harrison: *Suite for Symphonic Strings*
    A. Lanza: *Cuarteto V*
    S. Matsushita: *Fresque sonore*
    A. Mellnäs: *Gestes sonores; Per caso*
    K. M. Nazar: *Variazioni concertanti*
    K. Penderecki: *The Devils of Loudun; Fluorescences,* and other works
    A. de la Vega: *Segments for Violin and Piano; Structures for Piano and String Quartet*

Example 18 Mel Powell: from *Filigree Setting* (p. 2)

12. The player arpeggiates with the back of the bow across the four strings behind the bridge

M. Mitrea-Celarianu: *Seth*

13. The tailpiece is struck, tapped, or stroked *col legno;* the graphic symbol devised by Penderecki for this effect cannot be bettered: ♭

G. Burt: *Exit Music*
S. Bussotti: *Phrase à trois*
S. Cervetti: *Zinctum*
R. Gerhard: *Concert for 8; Concerto for Orchestra*
H-J. Hespos: *Passagen*
S. Hodkinson: *Fresco*
M. Ishi: *Aphorismen*
M. Kelemen: *Changeant; Surprise*
M. Mamiya: *String Quartet No. 1*
D. Martino: *Parisonatina al'dodecafonia*
K. Penderecki: *The Devils of Loudun; Polymorphia,* and other works
D. Reck: *Blues and Screamer*

14. *Col legno battuto* on the chin rest

R. Gerhard: *Concerto for Orchestra*

15. The undersides of the strings are rubbed with the wood of the bow just over the end of the fingerboard; the effect is obviously most feasible on cello and doublebass

B. Sakač: *Struktur I*

16. A tri-dimensional effect is obtained on cello by striking the two lower strings *col legno* while at the same time sliding the thumb and index finger on the strings, and plucking the C-string with the third or fourth finger

C. Alsina: *Trio 1967*

17. The doublebass player lightly stops the open strings to prevent clear pitches from sounding, the bow-wood bouncing from near the bridge to the fingerboard *(ricochet legno);* the aural result is a rapidly descending figure of indeterminate pitches

D. Bedford: *Music for Albion Moonlight; Piece for Mo*
J. Druckman: *Incenters; Valentine*

In addition to *col legno* there are a number of other and highly favored modes of percussive attack on the string(s) of the family members. In the listings that follow, the devices first enumerated apply to all the stringed instruments; those more or less limited to the cello and doublebass follow in separate listings. Certain manners of playing are only feasible on these latter instruments, owing to their size, shape, and the physical relationship of player to instrument. Devices applicable to all the instruments include:

1. Slap or strike the strings with the flat left-hand fingers over the fingerboard

    C. Alsina: *Trio 1967*

    G. Arrigo: *Infrarosa*

    D. Bedford: *Piece for Mo*

    S. Bussotti: *Mit einem gewissen sprechenden Ausdruck*

    F. Cerha: *Enjambments*

    S. Cervetti: *Six Sequences; Zinctum*

    D. Cope: *Angel's Camp II* (Example 38)

    A. Curran: *Home-made*

    M. Davidovsky: *Synchronisms No. 2*

    H-J. Hespos: *Passagen*

    M. Kagel: *Anagrama*

    M. Kelemen: *Changeant*

    W. Kilar: *Dipthongos*

    A. Mellnäs: *Aura*

    K. Meyer: *Concerto da Camera*

    P. Norgård: *Prism*

    K. Penderecki: *Dimensions of Time and Silence; Fluorescences,* and other works

    E. Raxach: *Estrofas*

    Z. Rudzinski: *Moments musicaux II*

    R. M. Schafer: *Requiems for the Party-Girl*

    B. Schäffer: *Scultura; String Quartet*

    H. Schramm: *Shilappadikaram*

    R. Sender: *Balances*

    W. Szalonek: *Concertino per flauto*

    K. E. Welin: *Nr.3-1961*

2. Same, with the left hand, across the bridge

    J. Fortner: *Quartet*

    R. M. Schafer: *Requiems for the Party-Girl*

    W. Sydeman: *Texture Studies*

3. Tap the string(s) with the left-hand finger(s)

    G. Becker: *Diaglyphen*

    S. Bussotti: *Il Nudo; Phrase à trois,* and other works

    F. Cerha: *Enjambments*

R. Haubenstock-Ramati: *Tableau*
A. Hrisanide: *Volumes*
M. Kagel: *Match; Sonant*
G. Ligeti: *Apparitions*
M. Mamiya: *String Quartet No. 1*
L. Nono: *Canti di vita e d'amore*
L. de Pablo: *Radial*
R. Reynolds: *Quick are the Mouths of Earth*
W. Sydeman: *Texture Studies*
W. Szalonek: *Concertino per flauto*
R. Wittinger: *Irreversibilitazione*

4. Trill on the strings with the left-hand fingers (no bow)
   M. Kupferman: *Infinities 24*

5. Tap on the string with a left-hand fingernail
   M. Davidovsky: *Synchronisms No. 3*

6. Tap on string with two right-hand fingers (quasi-trill)
   Y. Yannay: *preFIX-FIX-sufFIX*

7. Trill or tremolo with the fingernails of the right hand
   B. Rands: *Memo 1*

8. Tap on the string with a right-hand fingernail
   M. Subotnick: *Lamination I*
   W. Sydeman: *Projections I*

9. Tap the string(s) with the right-hand knuckles
   M. Kupferman: *Infinities 24*
   R. Sender: *Balances*

10. Strike open strings with palm of right hand
    S. Cervetti: *Six Sequences*
    A. Curran: *Home-made*
    M. Kagel: *Sonant*
    K. Meyer: *Concerto da Camera*

11. Slap the four strings across the bridge with the right-hand flat fingers
    W. Kotonski: *a battere*

12. Tap or trill with the right-hand fingers on the string(s) behind the bridge
    Z. Bujarski: *Kinoth*
    K. Penderecki: *Polymorphia*

13. Use both hands to slap strings quickly and loudly

    W. Sydeman: *Texture Studies*

14. Trill on the string(s) with two thimble-capped fingers

    G. Crumb: *Black Angels*

15. Tap on the string(s) with the ivory tip of the bow

    H. W. Henze: *Heliogabalus Imperator*
    P. Phillips: *Divertimento for Three String Basses*
    G. Read: *Symphony No. 3*

16. Use the metal (and wood) part of a pencil to bounce *(jeté)* on the string

    B. Schäffer: *String Quartet*
    W. Sydeman: *Projections I; Texture Studies,* and other works

17. Muffle the strings with the left hand; play on them with a pocket comb

    Y. Sadai: *Nuances*

18. Same, behind the bridge

    Y. Sadai: *Nuances*

19. Hold the instrument like a mandolin; strike the string with a glass rod held in the left hand; the open string sounds automatically as the rod rebounds from the string

    G. Crumb: *Black Angels*

Devices mainly applicable to cello and/or doublebass include:

1. Slap the four strings with the left-hand flat fingers near to or on the instrument neck

    I. Anhalt: *Foci*
    E. Kurtz: *Improvisation for Contrabass*

2. Roll on the strings with a mallet

    J. Druckman: *Valentine*
    L. Harrison: *Labyrinth No. 3*
    M. Kupferman: *Infinities 24*
    W. Sydeman: *Texture Studies*

3. Same, the mallets wielded by a percussionist

    G. Crumb: *Madrigals—I*

4. Drum on the strings with a pencil

    G. Rochberg: *Tableaux*

5. Same, with a metal stick

   H. Ebenhöh: *4 Szenen für 10*

6. Hit a string with a wooden stick; let it bounce while squeezing it against the string, creating a fast, tight roll

   J. Druckman: *Valentine*

7. Rattle a pencil, stick, or small dowel between two strings; close to the bridge this action picks up random harmonics

   B. Childs: *Mr. T., His Fancy*

8. Same, with the tip of the bow

   R. Aitken: *Kebyar*

9. Insert the handle of a mallet between two strings; beat rapidly from side to side while moving the handle from near the bridge to over the fingerboard

   J. Druckman: *Valentine*

10. Arpeggiate rapidly across the strings behind the bridge with a wooden stick

    J. Druckman: *Valentine*

    J. Yuasa: *Triplicity for Contrabass*

11. With a large wooden salad-tossing spoon in the left hand, strike the strings behind the bridge

    W. Sydeman: *Duo for Trumpet and Amplified Doublebass*

12. Same, with a tablespoon

    W. Sydeman: *Texture Studies*

13. Lay the doublebass flat between two padded supports; play on the open strings with two rods

    L. Harrison: *Violin Concerto*

14. Strike string(s) with a maraca

    D. Erb: *Reconnaisance*

For percussion on the body of a string instrument the player may, of course, employ the same agents used for striking the strings, plus additional objects listed below. Furthermore, the diversity of locale is quite extensive, particularly on cello and doublebass, whose surface areas are both larger and more easily accessible to the players than those of violin and viola. Though not all composers are as specific in pinpointing the areas to be struck as they are in designating the agent of attack, the areas available include the following: the fingerboard, front or belly, sides or ribs, back, top or shoulders, neck, nut, and scroll—as well as the more commonly designated bridge and tailpiece. The following is a fairly comprehensive cataloguing of the percussive effects possible on the body of a string instrument:

1. Knock, strike, or tap on the body of the instrument (exact locale unspecified by the composer) with the fingers or thumb

   C. Alsina: *Trio 1967*
   D. Bedford: *Gastrula*
   D. Burge: *Aeolian Music*
   S. Bussotti: *Il Nudo*
   S. Cervetti: *Six Sequences; Zinctum*
   B. Childs: *Nonet*
   G. Crumb: *Night Music II*
   M. Davidovsky: *Synchronisms No. 3*
   J. Druckman: *Incenters; Valentine,* and other works
   J. Fortner: *Quartet*
   A. Hrisanide: *Volumes*
   M. Ishi: *Aphorismen*
   M. Kagel: *Match*
   M. Kelemen: *Changeant*
   M. Kopelent: *3. Quartetto*
   A. Lanza: *Cuarteto V*
   T. Marco: *Aura*
   D. Martino: *Parisonatina al'dodecafonia*
   S. Matsushita: *Fresque sonore*
   B. Nilsson: *Versuchungen*
   K. Penderecki: *Capriccio per Siegfried Palm; Dimensions of Time and Silence,* and
        other works
   D. Reck: *Blues and Screamer*
   W. Rudzinski: *Pictures from the Holy-Cross Mountains*
   Y. Sadai: *Nuances*
   B. Schäffer: *4 Pieces for String Trio; Scultura,* and other works
   W. Szalonek: *Concertino per flauto*
   C. Whittenberg: *Conversations for Solo Double Bass*
   L. Widdoes: *From a Time of Snow*

2. Roll with the fingers, "quasi-tamburo," on the body (locale unspecified)

   J. Fortner: *S pr ING*
   A. Janson: *Canon*
   C. Whittenberg: *Conversations for Solo Double Bass*

3. Strike or tap on body of instrument (locale unspecified) with the fingernails

   R. Aitken: *Kebyar*
   D. Burge: *Aeolian Music*
   R. Haubenstock-Ramati: *Tableau*
   L. Widdoes: *From a Time of Snow*

4. Same, with the knuckles

   W. Albright: *Danse Macabre* (Example 17)
   D. Burge: *Aeolian Music*
   S. Cervetti: *Six Sequences; Zinctum*
   G. Crumb: *Black Angels; Echoes of Time and the River,* and other works
   W. Fortner: *Immagini*
   L. Hiller: *String Quartet No. 5*
   L. Hiller, L. M. Isaacson: *Illiac Suite*
   D. Reck: *Blues and Screamer*
   H. Schramm: *Schilappadikaram*
   W. Szalonek: *Concertino per flauto*
   D. Wilson: *Seventeen Views*

5. Same, with the flat hand

   C. Alsina: *Trio 1967* (Example 22)
   D. Burge: *Aeolian Music*
   C. Halffter: *Anillos*
   M. Kagel: *Match; Sonant*
   C. Whittenberg: *Conversations for Solo Double Bass*

6. Same, with the wood of the bow

   P. Chihara: *Driftwood*
   W. Fortner: *Immagini*
   A. Lanza: *Cuarteto V*
   B. Nilsson: *Versuchungen*
   D. Reck: *Blues and Screamer*
   Y. Sadai: *Nuances*

7. Same, with the nut (heel) of the bow

   K. Penderecki: *Dimensions of Time and Silence; Threnody,* and other works
   W. Rudzinski: *Pictures from the Holy-Cross Mountains*

8. Roll, tap, or trill with the fingers on the fingerboard

   A. Bancquart: *Ecorces III*
   G. Becker: *Diaglyphen*
   D. Bedford: *Five for String Quintet; Music for Albion Moonlight*

L. Berio: *Sinfonia*

A. Curran: *Home-made*

J. Druckman: *Incenters*

D. Erb: *String Trio*

J. Fortner: *Quartet*

R. Gerhard: *Concerto for Orchestra*

V. Globokar: *Accord*

C. Halffter: *Fibonaciana*

A. Hrisanide: *Volumes*

K. Huber: *Tenebrae*

D. Martino: *Parisonatina al' dodecafonia*

K. Penderecki: *Fluorescences; Polymorphia,* and other works

M. Powell: *Filigree Setting* (Example 18)

D. Reck: *Blues and Screamer*

W. Rudzinski: *Pictures from the Holy-Cross Mountains*

R. Sender: *Balances*

9. **Same, with the fingernails**

   R. Sender: *Balances*

10. **Same, with the knuckles**

    P. Chihara: *Logs*

11. **Same, with the bowhair**

    M. Davidovsky: *Synchronisms No. 3*

    E. Raxach: *Estrofas*

12. **Rub the fingerboard with the fingers or flat hand**

    A. Hrisanide: *Volumes*

    M. Ishi: *Aphorismen*

    K. Penderecki: *Fluorescences*

    W. Rudzinski: *Pictures from the Holy-Cross Mountains*

    B. Schäffer: *Scultura*

13. **Strike the fingerboard with the flat hand**

    I. Xenakis: *Pithoprakta*

14. **Same, with the cupped hand or fist**

    A. Bancquart: *Ecorces III*

    T. Fredrickson: *Music for Five Instruments*

15. **Snap the finger against the fingerboard**

    D. Erb: *Concerto for Solo Percussionist; The Seventh Trumpet*

16. Tap on the bridge with the finger(s)

    M. Kagel: *Match*
    K. Penderecki: *Capriccio per Siegfried Palm; String Quartet No. 2*

17. Same, with the hand

    M. Davidovsky: *Synchronisms No. 3*

18. Strike the bridge (of cello or doublebass) with a mallet, stick, or pencil

    B. Childs: *Nonet*

19. Tap horizontally on the bridge (between the strings) with the bowhair

    D. Bedford: *That White and Radiant Legend*
    J. Fortner: *Quartet*
    L. Harrison: *Suite for Symphonic Strings*
    S. Matsushita: *Fresque sonore*

20. Tap on the tailpiece with the finger(s)

    K. Huber: *Tenebrae*
    D. Martino: *Parisonatina al'dodecafonia*

21. Strike the tailpiece with the fingernail

    R. Sender: *Balances*

22. Rap, strike, or tap on the front (belly or box) of the instrument with the fingertips

    G. Burt: *Exit Music*
    B. Childs: *Mr. T., His Fancy*
    G. Crumb: *Madrigals—I; Night Music II*
    R. Gerhard: *Concerto for Orchestra*
    R. Goeb: *Fantasy for Oboe*
    L. Harrison: *Suite for Symphonic Strings*
    S. Hodkinson: *Interplay*
    D. Martino: *Parisonatina al'dodecafonia*
    P. Phillips: *Divertimento for Three String Basses*
    G. Rochberg: *Music for the Magic Theatre*
    R. Sender: *Balances*
    W. Sydeman: *Projections I*

23. Same, with the fingernails

    B. Childs: *Mr. T., His Fancy*
    R. Sender: *Balances*

24. Same, with the knuckles

   S. Cervetti: *Zinctum*
   B. Childs: *Mr. T., His Fancy*
   G. Crumb: *Night of the Four Moons*
   R. Gerhard: *String Quartet No. 2*
   E. Kurtz: *Improvisation for Contrabass*

25. Same, with the flat hand

   E. Kurtz: *Improvisation for Contrabass*
   K. Penderecki: *Capriccio per Oboe*

26. Same, with cupped hand

   T. Fredrickson: *Music for Five Instruments*

27. Same, with the bowstick

   S. Cervetti: *Zinctum*

28. Tap on rim of the side and belly with the tip of the bow, moving toward the scroll

   W. Sydeman: *Texture Studies*

29. Tap on one side of the instrument with the fingertips

   B. Childs: *Mr. T., His Fancy*
   M. Kagel: *Match*

30. Same, with the fingernails

   T. Baird: *Espressioni varianti* (Example 19)
   P. Chihara: *Logs*
   B. Childs: *Mr. T., His Fancy*
   R. Erickson: *Ricercar à 3*

31. Same, with the thumb

   B. Childs: *Mr. T., His Fancy*

32. Same, with the knuckles

   D. Burge: *Aeolian Music*
   F. Cerha: *Enjambments*
   P. Chihara: *Logs*
   B. Childs: *Mr. T., His Fancy*
   A. Curran: *Home-made*
   A. de la Vega: *Structures for Piano and String Quartet*

Example 19   Tadeusz Baird: from *Espressioni varianti* (p. 31)

*) uderzać paznokciem w bok instrumentów
Frapper avec l'ongle le côté de l'instrument

33. **Same, with the bowstick**

    H. Haufrecht: *Square Set*

34. **Same, with a pencil**

    B. Childs: *Mr. T., His Fancy*

35. **Rub ("caress") the side of the doublebass**

    J. Deak: *Color Studies for Contrabass*

36. **Rub back of the rib (of doublebass), producing a high squeak**

    J. Deak: *Color Studies for Contrabass*

37. **Strike or tap on the back of the instrument with the fingers or thumb**

    P. Chihara: *Logs*
    T. Fredrickson: *Music for Five Instruments*
    L. Harrison: *Suite for Symphonic Strings*
    K. Huber: *Tenebrae*

M. Powell: *Filigree Setting* (Example 18)

I. Xenakis: *ST/4-1, 080262*

38. Same, with the knuckles

    T. Fredrickson: *Music for Five Instruments*

    C. Santoro: *3 Abstrações*

    A. de la Vega: *Structures for Piano and String Quartet*

39. Same, with the flat hand

    D. Cope: *Angel's Camp II* (Example 38)

    M. Subotnick: *Lamination I*

40. Same, with the bowstick *(col legno)*

    B. Sakač: *Struktur I*

41. Same, with a timpani stick (on doublebass)

    Y. Sadai: *Nuances*

42. Rattle fingernails against the back of the instrument

    D. Erb: *The Seventh Trumpet*

43. Turn the instrument over (violin or viola) and strike on the center of the back with the flat hand

    I. Xenakis: *ST/4-1, 080262*

44. Slap, strike, or tap on the top (shoulders) of the instrument (cello or doublebass) with the cupped hand

    R. Erickson: *Ricercar à 3*

    K. Gaburo: *Inside*

45. Same, with the fingernails

    R. Erickson: *Ricercar à 3*

    K. Gaburo: *Inside*

46. Same, with the left-hand fingers

    K. Gaburo: *Inside*

    I. Lang: *Impulsioni*

    D. Martino: *Parisonatina al' dodecafonia*

47. Strike scroll with the finger(s)

    R. Sender: *Balances*

48. Same, with the fingernail(s)

    R. Sender: *Balances*

49. Snap the fingernail on the back of the instrument neck

    B. Childs: *Nonet*

Indubitably a percussive device, though not effected on the instrument body, is the stipulation to strike or tap rhythmically on the music stand with the bowtip *(col legno)*, this appears in:

G. Burt: *Exit Music*
V. Globokar: *Accord*
K. Penderecki: *Fluorescences; Polymorphia*
R. M. Schafer: *Requiems for the Party-Girl*
W. Szalonek: *Concertino per flauto*

This practice (the traditional, but dubious, interpretation of the *"col legno"* directive in Rossini's 1813 overture to *Il Signor Bruschino*) is related to another avant-garde device: the player lightly strikes his chair with the nut of the bow. This is an alternative action for the music-stand tappings in the Penderecki works mentioned above.

It does not seem likely that the ultimate of percussive potential of the strings—indeed, of all nonpercussion instruments—has been discovered, let alone exploited by the avant-garde composer of the late twentieth century. Predictions are suspect, but one ventures to say that in the years to come experimentally minded composers will bring to light new and intriguing ways in which to coax percussive sounds from the standard instruments, as well as to foster novel percussive effects on instruments yet to be invented.

6

MICROTONES

Woodwinds and Brasses

Microtonal pitch inflection is a staple of the current avant-garde in both instrumental and vocal music. Formerly restricted to the string instruments and sparingly used even in the serious music of the early twentieth century, quarter-tones and even smaller subdivisions of the half-step are now an integral part of wind-instrument techniques. Though few works by our Western composers are restricted solely to microtonal pitch inflection (as, for instance, Julian Carrilo's orchestral *Preludio a Colón* and the *Cuarteto en ¼ de tono*, and several of the string quartets of Alois Hába), quarter-tone "bends" and glissandi are now fairly common phenomena in recent vanguard scores.[1]

Microtonal bends—the gradual flatting or sharping of a given note—are achieved by the woodwinds through the embouchure, the lip pressure being tightened or relaxed according to the designated direction of the minute pitch inflection. Flute players generally roll the instrument slowly away from the lips, for upward bends, or into the lips, for downward bends, thus minutely altering

[1] According to Bruno Bartolozzi (in his *New Sounds for Woodwind*) quarter-tones are now possible on the four standard woodwinds as follows: flute—from d¹ to g♯³; oboe—c¹ to f♯³; clarinet—a♯ to g♯³; and bassoon—E to d².

the degree and angle of the air stream directed into the mouthpiece. This action affects the blown and fingered pitch, causing it to rise or sink by a quarter-tone, a third-tone, or other designated fractional interval, according to the distance the instrument is moved. Shown below are a few of the many symbols recently invented for microtonal wind-instrument bends (ascending):

Among a great many contemporary works requiring some kind of micro-tonal inflection (bends, glissandi, and the like) we might cite:

1. Flute and/or alto flute

W. Albright: *Danse Macabre*

Z. Bujarski: *Chamber Piece*

S. Bussotti: *Couple*

Chou Wen-chung: *Cursive*

M. Colgrass: *As Quiet As*

G. Crumb: *Eleven Echoes of Autumn* (Example 30); *Night of the Four Moons,* and other works

L. Foss: *For 24 Winds*

H. Gaber: *Voce II*

B. Hambraeus: *Introduzione, Sequenze, Coda*

J. Heiss: *Movements for Three Flutes*

H. W. Henze: *El Cimarron; Sinfonia N. 6*

G. Heussenstamm: *Poikilos*

S. Hodkinson: *Fresco; Interplay,* and other works

K. Korte: *Remembrances*

W. Kotonski: *Musica per fiati e timpani*

H. Kox: *Cyclofonie V*

J. Mekeel: *The Shape of Silence*

K. Penderecki: *De Natura Sonoris (I)*

C. Polin: *The Death of Procris*

G. Read: *Sonoric Fantasia No. 3*

D. Reck: *Blues and Screamer*

R. Reynolds: *Ambages; Traces,* and other works

G. Rochberg: *Music for the Magic Theatre; Tableaux,* and other works

W. Rudzinski: *Pictures from the Holy-Cross Mountains*

B. Schäffer: *Azione a due*

G. Schuller: *Contours; Seven Studies on Themes of Paul Klee,* and other works
E. Schwartz: *Texture*
H. Sollberger: *Grand Quartet for Flutes*
T. Takemitsu: *Masque for two Flutes; Voice*
L. Widdoes: *From a Time of Snow*
B. A. Zimmermann: *Photoptosis; Tempus loquendi*

2. Recorder

W. Heider: *Katalog*

3. Oboe and/or English horn

T. Antoniou: *Five Likes*
B. Bartolozzi: *Concertazioni per oboe*
L. Berio: *Sequenza VII*
B. Childs: *Four Inventions; Four Involutions,* and other works
G. Crumb: *Ancient Voices of Children*
L. Foss: *For 24 Winds*
W. Kotonski: *Musica per fiati e timpani*
K. Penderecki: *De Natura Sonoris (I)*
R. Reynolds: *Quick are the Mouths of Earth*
G. Schuller: *Seven Studies on Themes of Paul Klee*
W. Sydeman: *Texture Studies*
I. Yun: *Dimensionen*
B. A. Zimmermann: *Photoptosis*

4. Clarinet and/or bass clarinet

G. Crumb: *Eleven Echoes of Autumn*
L. Foss: *For 24 Winds*
H. W. Henze: *Sinfonia N. 6*
W. Kotonski: *Pour quatre*
D. Martino: *Strata*
G. Rochberg: *Music for the Magic Theatre*
W. Sydeman: *Texture Studies*
I. Xenakis: *Polytope*
B. A. Zimmermann: *Photoptosis*

5. Saxophone

H. W. Henze: *Sinfonia N. 6*
K. Husa: *Apotheosis of This Earth*
C. Polin: *O, Aderyn Pur*

6. Bassoon and/or contrabassoon

P. Chihara: *Branches*
L. Foss: *For 24 Winds*
H. W. Henze: *Sinfonia N. 6*
K. Penderecki: *De Natura Sonoris (I)*
I. Xenakis: *Polytope*
B. A. Zimmermann: *Photoptosis*

A slight change in normal embouchure is usually sufficient to produce microtonal bends on the horn; the effect can also be obtained by partial hand-stopping. On trumpet, quarter-tone inflections are produced by adjustments of the tuning slides, and on trombone by maneuvering the slide between positions. Embouchure adjustment takes care of microtonal inflections on tuba.

The following scores all require the use of these techniques on the various brass instruments:

1. Horn

G. Crumb: *Echoes of Time and the River*
D. Erb: *Symphony of Overtures*
V. Globokar: *Etude pour Folklora II*
K. Huber: *Tenebrae*
W. Kotonski: *Musica per fiati e timpani*
L. Nono: *Canti di vita e d'amore*
K. Penderecki: *Dies Irae*
G. Rochberg: *Tableaux*
W. Szalonek: *Aarhus Music*
I. Xenakis: *Akrata; Metataseis,* and other works
B. A. Zimmermann: *Photoptosis*

2. Trumpet

N. T. Dao: *Phū-Dông*
D. Erb: *Symphony of Overtures*
W. Kotonski: *Musica per fiati e timpani*
L. Nono: *Canti di vita e d'amore*
I. Xenakis: *Eonta* (Example 20); *Polytope*
B. A. Zimmerman: *Photoptosis*

3. Trombone

L. Austin: *Changes*
B. Childs: *Jack's New Bag*

4. Tuba

An effect allied to the microtonal bend, available to both woodwind and brass instruments, is the quarter-tone vibrato: the player's normal vibrato is exaggerated to the extent that an actual quarter-tone "beat" is perceived (as in

Example 20   Iannis Xenakis: from *Eonta* (p. 39)

*Vibrato avec la coulisse le plus rapide possible entre les notes rectangulaires et suivant les rythmes indiqués, les notes extrèmes des oscillations variant d'une manière continue.

Husa's *Apotheosis of this Earth*). A wide vibrato on the trombone, produced by slide action, can also create a microtonal wavering of pitch (required in the *Eonta* and *Metastaseis* of Xenakis, for example).

Furthermore, many composers request passages of unstable pitch, timbre, and/or frequency from their wind players. Unstable pitch would be accomplished by liberal recourse to microtonal bendings, while unstable timbre results from a flexible mixing of tonguing techniques, embouchure control (irregular pressure of lips and varied breath force), fingering variants, and rapid alternations of degrees of vibrato and non-vibrato. These requirements form a conspicuous part of the technical procedures in Earle Brown's *Available Forms 1 and 2.*

To date composers have not notably exploited the possibilities of consistent microtonal tunings of the brass instruments, either individually or sectionally. Only a handful of recent experimental works exhibit this special tonal concept, such as Alcides Lanza's *Eidesis II,* in which the second players of horn and trombone are to tune their instruments a quarter-tone flat in relation to the instruments of the first players.

Harp and Other Plucked Instruments

Few twentieth-century works, to date, have required microtonal harp tunings; Sylvano Bussotti's *Fragmentations* for two harps, one tuned unconventionally, and Alain Banquart's orchestral *Palimpsestes* are the most notable examples of this tuning procedure.[2] Quarter-tone bends, however, can be created on normally tuned harp strings; they are produced in two ways: first, the tuning key may be lightly pressed against a string to be plucked and then moved slowly up or down the string (as in Harrison Birtwistle's *Entr' actes and Sappho Fragments*). Second, the left hand presses hard against the plucked string quite close to the tuning pins (as specified in George Crumb's *Ancient Voices of Children* and in Vinko Globokar's *Voie*).

Quarter-tone slides have also been requisitioned of guitar and mandolin by certain vanguardists. They are accomplished on these plucked instruments by pulling the string laterally with a left-hand finger immediately after the string is plucked normally with the right hand (see Crumb's work just cited and Lukas Foss's *Fragments of Archilochos*). Quarter-tone trills on these instruments are

---

[2]Most theorists know, of course, that Julian Carrillo's 1922 *Preludio a Colón* includes a part for a harp specially tuned in 16th-tones; the work, however, was not published until 1969, so remained largely unknown to composers.

in reality vibratos of such width that a microtonal pitch variance can be perceived (also specified in Crumb's score).

Keyboard Instruments

Even in the highly experimental milieu of late twentieth-century composition, the use of quarter-tone piano is comparatively rare. The early microtonal experiments of Hába, Hans Barth, and Carrillo, which led to the construction of keyboard instruments capable of producing quarter-tones, did not create a sizable corresponding body of literature for these innovative instruments. Aside from a few works by these three composers, and some occasional oddities such as the *Three Quarter-Tone Pieces* of Charles Ives, we lack a significant corpus of keyboard microtonal music. It is, therefore, a novelty of some note when one comes across such a work as Donald Lybbert's *Lines for the Fallen,* which requires that one of its two pianos be tuned a quarter-tone low. Also, in Jean-Etienne Marie's *Tombeau de Julian Carrillo,* one of two pianos required is—appropriately enough—tuned a third-tone higher than the other.

If there are any instances of microtonal tunings of harpsichord, celesta, or organ, they are unknown to this author.

Strings

String players have long produced minute differences in notated pitch by means of wide vibrato or by finger and position shifting on enharmonic tones (G♭ and F♯, for example). But such fractional colorings of pitch were never actually specified by the composers until the early twentieth century, when microtones became an integral part of string technique—especially quarter-tones, which are both theoretically and practically the most feasible. Spurred by the experiments of such theorists as Carrillo and Hába, and espoused by composers as diverse in style as Alban Berg, Ernest Bloch, and Béla Bartók, string instrument microtones are now designated by orchestrators with increasing frequency.

Some vanguardists conceive of microtones as the basis of an entirely new scale format (as Harry Partch's 43-tone scale, for example); the majority employ them purely as coloristic agents, to modify or to enhance existing pitches in the traditional chromatic scale.

The most common usage by far of microtonal variance within the twelve-note system is the quarter-tone vibrato: the player produces a slow and greatly exaggerated vibrato on his instrument in which pitches a quarter-tone above or below (or both) the principal tone can be readily heard. The requisite notation devised by Penderecki in *Fluorescences* and other scores is clear and succinct:

Among many recent works calling for quarter-tone vibratos are:

S. Cervetti: *Zinctum*
L. Foss: *Echoi; Elytres*
A. Hrisanide: *Volumes*
K. Huber: *Alveare vernat*
M. Kagel: *Match; Sexteto de cuerdas,* and other works
A. Mellnäs: *Quasi nienti*
P. Norgård: *Symphony No. 2*
K. Penderecki: *Emanationen; Miniatures,* and other works

Quarter- or third-tone glissandi of brief extent are other ways in which minute pitch fluctuations can be achieved on strings, the finger sliding almost imperceptibly up or down from normal full or half position; such requirements appear in:

D. Bedford: *That White and Radiant Legend*
J. Deak: *Color Studies for Contrabass*
F. Evangelisti: *Aleatorio*
K. Penderecki: *Emanationen*
D. Reck: *Blues and Screamer*
G. Rochberg: *Duo Concertante*
W. Sydeman: *Texture Studies*
R. Wittinger: *Quartetto per archi No. 3*

In his *Incenters* Jacob Druckman requests a trill a quarter-tone both above and below a specified pitch; the result is what he aptly describes as a "whimpering and whining sound." Quarter-tone bends are produced by the doubleblass player in George Crumb's *Madrigals—IV* by turning slightly the tuning peg of the string played, rather than by finger shifting.

Just as quarter-tone "beats" can be produced on single woodwind instruments playing certain multiphonic structures (see page 146), so can microtonal beating tones be created by individual stringed instruments playing double-stopped unisons, the higher of the two strings fingered a quarter-tone above the lower string. This action is called for, and with striking results, in Peter Maxwell Davies' *Revelation and Fall.*

Xenakis in *Nomos* calls for a quarter-tone inflection to be produced in a curious manner: the cellist stops G on the C-string with his first finger, then plucks the string with his thumb between the instrument nut and the finger on the string; the resultant sound is an octave higher plus a quarter-tone.

It is an odd fact that few composers have required preperformance tunings of the strings in microtones, either of individual instruments or of whole sections within the string choir. So far only three instances have come to light: György Ligeti's *Ramifications for Double String Orchestra,* in which the violins, violas, and cellos of one orchestra are tuned a quarter-tone higher than those of the other orchestra; Alcides Lanza's *Eidesis II,* which requires one cello to be pretuned a quarter-tone high and one cello and one doublebass a quarter-tone low; and *Monodram* of Henryk Gorecki, in which only the doublebasses are to pretune all four of their strings down, possibly exceeding a quarter-tone.

In due time the present paucity of examples of microtonal string orchestra tuning will no doubt be augmented as more orchestrators discover the timbral benefits to be gained from using this special technique.

7

AMPLIFICATION

In modern music-making the most obvious manifestation of electronic technology is tape recorder, synthesizer, and computer composition. But the basic science and various techniques of electronic sound manipulation have also affected nonelectronic music, mainly through live performance amplification. Contact microphones can be attached to certain instruments, or the players can direct their instrumental sounds into individual air microphones placed directly before them, suspended above them, or attached to their bodies. Normal amplitudes can thus be increased—even distorted—and characteristic timbres radically altered through the use of special filters (ring modulators) connected to the amplifiers. Microphones and amplifiers are, of course, hooked into one or more loudspeakers placed in different locations in the performance area. Spatial, or stereophonic, impressions are thus directed to the individual listeners, wherever they may be located in the auditorium.

Electronic amplification of instruments (or voices) is motivated by two factors: first, to obtain simple volume control of normal instrumental or vocal tone; second, to achieve radical timbral alteration. Among the several possibilities for tone-color manipulation are: feedback, distortion, reverberation, time-lapse, and the splitting of pitches through ring modulators. All have become viable new sound resources, independent of prerecorded or simultaneous tapings.[1]

Woodwinds and Brasses

As with any instrument of the symphonic orchestra or band, the woodwinds and brasses can be individually or collectively amplified by the procedures just described. Recent compositions, mostly of an experimental nature, requiring woodwind instrument amplification include the following:

1. Flute

   H. Birtwistle: *Nomos*
   G. Crumb: *Vox Balaenae*
   B. Hambraeus: *Introduzione, Sequenze, Coda*
   T. Takemitsu: *Voice*

2. Bass flute

   P. Chihara: *Willow, Willow*

3. Bass recorder

   L. Andriessen: *Hoe het is*

4. Oboe

   H. Holliger: *Siebengesang*

5. Clarinet

   H. Birtwistle: *Nomos*

6. Saxophone

   D. Del Tredici: *Pop-Pourri*

7. Bassoon

   H. Birtwistle: *Nomos*

Scores that call for brass instrument amplification include:

---

[1]Although primarily discussing doublebass amplification, Chapter VII of Bertram Turetzky's *The Contemporary Contrabass* is a comprehensive discussion of instrumental amplification in all its aspects.

1. Horn

   H. Birtwistle: *Nomos*

   G. Mumma: *Hornpipe* (the horn played with a bassoon reed!)

2. Trombone

   W. Heider: *-einander*

Percussion

Because most percussion instruments are inherently loud, few composers have called for their electronic amplification. Nonetheless, there are one or two quite recent works, highly exploratory in intent, that do require amplification of certain of the percussion instruments; they are:

1. Vibraphone

   P. Chihara: *Willow, Willow* (amplified through a conventional air microphone connected to an Echo-plex)

2. Tubular bells

   B. Hambraeus: *Introduzione, Sequenze, Coda*

3. Marimbula (African harp)

   H. W. Henze: *Heliogabalus Imperator*

4. Cymbals

   K. Stockhausen: *Mixtur*

5. Tam-tam

   R. O'Donnell: *Microtimbre I*

   K. Stockhausen: *Hymnen; Kurzwellen; Mikrophonie I, II; Mixtur; Prozession*

Cymbals, gongs, and tam-tams customarily have contact microphones taped onto their surfaces, tightly enough so that they do not rattle against the surface when the instrument is struck.

To date, the most notable example of percussion amplification occurs in Jani Christou's *Enantiodromia:* a separated group of percussion instruments consisting of tubular bells, gongs, sizzle cymbals, and bass drum (all amplified) are reserved for an impressive entry at the work's climax. In the composer's words: "When they are struck, the collective impact should result in an almost deafening explosion, capable of cutting through the full orchestra playing at its maximum loudness." Doubtless!

Harp and Other Plucked Instruments

Instances of amplified harp are few, indeed; research has brought to light only five compositions requiring this technological aid:

A. Boucourechliev: *Anarchipel and Archipel 5*
M. Constant: *Candide*
P. M. Davies: *Revelation and Fall*
P. Méfano: *La Cérémonie*
P. Norgård: *Symphony No. 2*

Electric guitars are, of course, staple ingredients of rock music, but amplification of the guitar in serious orchestral and chamber music is also an accepted modus operandi among vanguard composers, such as:

G. Crumb: *Songs, Drones, and Refrains of Death*
D. Del Tredici: *Pop-Pourri*
D. Erb: *String Trio*
L. Foss: *Fragments of Archilochos; Paradigm*
H. W. Henze: *Sinfonia N. 6* (also banjo)
S. Hodkinson: *Fresco*
M. Kagel: *Sonant*
A. Mellnäs: *Tombola*
K. Penderecki: *Partita*
E. Raxach: *Interface*
K. Stockhausen: *Gruppen*
T. Takemitsu: *Cassiopeia*
J. Tavener: *Celtic Requiem*
C. Wolff: *Electric Spring I, II, III*

Keyboard Instruments

Certain recent scores have called for amplification of both piano and harpsichord. Contact microphones can be attached to certain preselected interior strings, as in Mestres-Quadreny's *Double Concerto* and in Crumb's *Songs,*

Drones, and Refrains of Death and *Vox Balaenae* (both using piano). They may also be placed in such a position in the piano or harpsichord interior as to pick up the vibrations of any or all of the struck or plucked strings; see, among other works:

I. Anhalt: *Foci*

L. Austin: *The Maze*

D. Bedford: *Come in here child*

A. Boucourechliev: *Anarchipel and Archipel 5* (cembalo)

M. Constant: *Quatorze Stations*

G. Crumb: *Makrokosmos—Vol. I*

J. Fulkerson: *Now II* (clavichord)

H. W. Henze: *Compasses*

B. Kolb: *Trobar Clus*

K. Penderecki: *Partita*

G. Rochberg: *Electrakaleidoscope; Tableaux*

Y. Takahashi: *Bridges I*

Strings

Amplification has been applied to various string instruments, quite generally in a solo context or in chamber music ensemble, in the following recent scores:

1. Violin

M. Constant: *Candide*

P. M. Davies: *Revelation and Fall*

H. W. Henze: *Sinfonia N. 6*

R. Laneri: *L'Arte del Violino*

W. Sydeman: *Projections I*

Y. Takahashi: *Rosace I*

C. Wuorinen: *Concerto for Amplified Violin*

Two contact microphones, one taped to the instrument body and one attached to the bowhair (!), are specified in Roberto Laneri's tongue-in-cheek work listed. And in Wuorinen's solo concerto a transducer, which is built into the violin bridge, is connected to a pre-amplifier controlled by an offstage technician.

2. Viola

   K. Stockhausen: *Hymnen; Kurzwellen,* and other works

3. Cello

   M. Constant: *Candide*
   G. Crumb: *Night of the Four Moons; Vox Balaenae*
   Y. Takahashi: *Bridges I*

4. Doublebass

   A. Bloch: *Gilgamesz*
   P. Chihara: *Logs*
   G. Crumb: *Songs, Drones, and Refrains of Death*
   P. M. Davies: *Revelation and Fall*
   K. Huber: *Tenebrae*
   M. Karlins: *Reflux*
   P. Méfano: *Lignes*
   B. Rands: *Memo 1*
   W. Sydeman: *Duo for Trumpet and Amplified Doublebass*

Bernard Rands is very specific as to amplification procedures in *Memo 1* : "A contact microphone should be firmly attached to the body of the instrument—preferably just in front of the bridge. This should be connected to an amplifier and two speakers placed stereophonically either side of the instrumentalist and as far away from him as is practicable. A foot pedal should be used to control the amplitude. The instrument should be placed as far away from the amplifer as possible to prevent feedback."

5. String Quartet

   G. Crumb: *Black Angels*

In Crumb's unusual score the composer specifies instruments with a built-in pick-up, but indicates that conventional instruments with contact microphones attached to their bellies with rubber bands would be acceptable substitutes.

Performance amplification of the standard orchestral and ensemble instruments is a new compositional device that is not invariably successful. Although one of the primary reasons for instrumental amplification is to produce a certain distortion of the instrument's normal tone, amplifying its sound often creates unwanted falsification of timbre as well as conspicuous dynamic imbalance. To put the matter bluntly, the composer must be aware of the often unpredictable behavior of amplification systems. Furthermore, he must prejudge whether unexpected degrees of electronic amplification during performance might help or harm his expression. He must determine whether novelty of amplified instrumental sound is worth the hazards of its technical production. If it is, of course he need have no reservations in applying this recent technological accommodation to his music.

8

EXTRAMUSICAL DEVICES

The concepts of multimedia—in particular those pertaining to such avant-garde manifestations as Happenings, The Living Theatre, and similar experimental approaches to staging—directly influence a considerable body of vanguard musical expression today. Such music is not content to rely on aural perception alone from its listeners but demands visual, even tactile, communication as well to put its total message across. Indeed, the listener to much avant-garde music is required to be an active participant in extramusical activities.

It is not strange, then, that experimental compositions of the late twentieth century often demand a certain degree of theatricality from the performers—extracurricular activities, as it were, that include emphatic and exaggerated bodily movement, visible facial contortion, perambulation during performance, and vocal projection independent of instrumental playing. These concepts of performance cut right across the board; they are not confined to any one type or kind of instrumentalist (or singer), nor do they require special idiomatic attributes from any of the players involved other than a minimum sense of dramatics and a willingness to participate in such supra-musical requirements.

Whether the unconventional activities expected by the composer help or hinder the player in his labors, loosen up his reflexes or inhibit them, engage his lively interest or embarrass him, are moot points. But as theatricalities, perambulations, vocalizations, and related performance activities are basic to our avant-garde milieu, the instrumentalist and singer of today has to participate as wholeheartedly as he is able in the convincing performance of such new music.

The categories that follow represent the most commonly demanded extra-musical activities found in current scores:

1. Instrumentalists are sometimes directed in their parts to stand up to play—as often, perhaps, for acoustical as for histrionic reasons. Not even cellists and harpist are exempt from this stipulation, in spite of the physical awkwardness involved. Directives to stand while playing occur in:

Woodwinds

D. Bedford: *Pentomino* (quintet)
B. Rands: *Ballad I* (flute)

Brasses

H. Birtwistle: *Verses for Ensemble* (horns)
J. Christou: *Enantiodromia* (all brasses)
E. Schwartz: *Music for Napoleon and Beethoven* (trumpet)
I. Xenakis: *Eonta* (trumpets; trombones)

Plucked instruments

G. Crumb: *Echoes of Time and the River* (mandolin)
R. Felciano: *Background Music* (harp)

Strings

L. Berio: *Epifanie* (solo violins)
J. Christou: *Enantiodromia* (a few violins)
L. Foss: *Orpheus* (solo cello)
F. Miroglio: *Projections* (solo violin; viola)

2. Perambulation, from off- to on-stage, or the reverse, or around the concert platform or the auditorium itself, is an integral and indispensable factor in the following works:

Woodwinds

I. Anhalt: *Foci*
W. Bolcomb: *Duets for Quintet*
D. Burge: *Sources III*
J. Cage: *Variations IV*
G. Crumb: *Echoes of Time and the River*
L. Foss: *Echoi; Orpheus*

M. Kelemen: *Entrances*

T. de Leeuw: *Spatial Music IV*

J. Mekeel: *The Shape of Silence*

Brasses

I. Anhalt: *Foci*

G. Crumb: *Echoes of Time and the River*

V. Globokar: *Discours II*

E. Schwartz: *Music for Napoleon and Beethoven* (Example 21); *Options I*

I. Xenakis: *Eonta*

Percussion

L. Austin: *The Maze*

Keyboard Instruments

E. Schwartz: *Music for Napoleon and Beethoven* (Example 21)

Strings

I. Anhalt: *Foci*

W. Bolcomb: *Duets for Quintet*

T. de Leeuw: *Spatial Music IV*

F. Miroglio: *Projections*

W. Sydeman: *Projections I*

For percussionists, perambulation has severe limitations. The players of timpani, gongs and tam-tam, and the idiophones, for example, can hardly be expected to function normally while moving about the concert platform. But the smaller and more portable instruments—woodblock, triangle, tambourine, maracas, finger cymbals, and the like—can all be played easily and effectively while the percussionist is moving about.

Keyboard players cannot, quite obviously, stroll about while performing. But one composer, at least, has directed his pianist to perform other functions while walking about. In Elliott Schwartz's *Music for Napoleon and Beethoven*, the pianist is required to get up from the keyboard and to circle about the solo trumpeter, who stands close to the piano. Each time the pianist passes in front of the trumpet bell he is to insert, or to remove, one of three different mute types which he carries in his hand. Before returning to the keyboard he obligingly turns the page for the trumpeter. (Example 21).

Rather elaborate scenarios of movement, including exchanging one seat for another, are found in Harrison Birtwistle's *Verses for Ensemble* and in George Crumb's orchestral *Echoes of Time and the River*. All stage action on

Example 21   Elliott Schwartz: from *Music for Napoleon and Beethoven* (p. 6)

the part of performers must be carefully plotted by the composer lest unnecessary collision and/or confusion result from haphazard movement.

3. Vocalizations of one kind or another—speaking, shouting, screaming, whistling, hissing, grunting, muttering, laughing, whispering, singing, humming—either completely independent of instrumental playing or else combined with various methods of sound production on the instruments, have been demanded with increasing frequency of performers, as in:

Woodwinds

D. Bedford: *Music for Albion Moonlight*

B. Childs: *Nonet*

D. Cope: *Indices*

G. Crumb: *Echoes of Time and the River; Eleven Echoes of Autumn,* and other works

L. Foss: *Paradigm*

S. Hodkinson: *Fresco*

K. Husa: *Apotheosis of this Earth*

B. Rands: *Wildtrack 1*

D. Reck: *Blues and Screamer*

R. M. Schafer: *Requiems for the Party-Girl*

T. Takemitsu: *Voice*

Brasses

R. Aitken: *Kebyar*

C. Alsina: *Trio 1967* (Example 22)

J. Bark, F. Rabe: *Bolos*

G. Burt: *Exit Music*

B. Childs: *Nonet*

N. T. Dao: *Phū-Dông*[1]

M. Ellis: *Mutations*

D. Erb: *The Seventh Trumpet*

V. Globokar: *Discours II*

S. Hodkinson: *Fresco*

A. Lanza: *Eidesis II*

P. Patterson: *Rebecca*

E. Schwartz: *Music for Napoleon and Beethoven* (Example 21); *Rip,* and other works

Percussion

L. Berio: *Circles*

B. Childs: *Jack's New Bag; Nonet,* and other works

[1]The horn player is directed to speak into the bell of the instrument.

G. Crumb: *Echoes of Time and the River; Eleven Echoes of Autumn,* and other works

L. Foss: *Paradigm*

J. Hawkins: *Three Cavatinas*

M. Kagel: *Sonant*

A. Lanza: *Eidesis II*

B. Rands: *Ballad I; Wildtrack 1*

E. Raxach: *Paraphrase*

Harp and Other Plucked Instruments

L. Foss: *Paradigm*

M. Kagel: *Sonant*

B. Rands: *Wildtrack 1*

R. M. Schafer: *Requiems for the Party-Girl*

Keyboard Instruments

D. Burge: *A Song of Sixpence; Sources III*

B. Childs: *Jack's New Bag; Nonet,* and other works

G. Crumb: *Echoes of Time and the River; Eleven Echoes of Autumn* (Example 30), and other works

B. Rands: *Ballad I*

R. M. Schafer: *Requiems for the Party-Girl*

B. Schäffer: *Musica per pianoforte*

E. Schwartz: *Music for Prince Albert*

K. Stockhausen: *Refrain*

Strings

D. Bedford: *Music for Albion Moonlight*

B. Childs: *Jack's New Bag; Mr. T., His Fancy,* and other works

J. Christou: *Enantiodromia*

D. Cope: *Angel's Camp II* (Example 38); *Cedar Breaks,* and other works

G. Crumb: *Black Angels; Madrigals—I,* and other works

J. Deak: *Color Studies for Contrabass; Surrealist Studies*

D. Erb: *Trio for Two*

R. Erickson: *Ricercar à 3*

R. Felciano: *Spectra*

J. Fortner: *Quartet*

L. Foss: *Paradigm*

G. Heussenstamm: *Pentalogue*

M. Kagel: *Sonant*

A. Lanza: *Eidesis II*

P. Oliveros: *Doublebasses at Twenty Paces*

R. Peck: *Automobile; 1 db(1968)*

K. Penderecki: *Fluorescences; Polymorphia*

F. Rabe: *Pajazzo*

B. Rands: *Ballad I; Wildtrack 1,* and other works

D. Reck: *Night Sounds (and Dream)*

G. Rochberg: *Tableaux*

R. M. Schafer: *Requiems for the Party-Girl*

E. Schwartz: *Dialogue for Solo Contrabass*

R. Whittenberg: *Conversations for Solo Double Bass*

4. Exaggerated body movements, facial contortions, and calculated theatrical gestures of one kind or another—foot stamping, finger snapping, hand clapping, and the like—supplement the performance contributions of various instrumentalists in the following scores:

Woodwinds

B. Childs: *Nonet*

R. Felciano: *Contractions*

Example 22 Carlos Alsina: from *Trio 1967* (p. 9)

V. Globokar: *Discours III*
S. Hodkinson: *Fresco*
B. Rands: *Ballad I*

Brasses

R. Aitken: *Kebyar*
C. Alsina: *Consequenza; Trio 1967* (Example 22)
B. Childs: *Nonet*
N. T. Dao: *Phū-Dồng*
M. Ellis: *Mutations*
S. Hodkinson: *Fresco*
A. Mellnäs: *Tombola*
E. Schwartz: *Music for Napoleon and Beethoven* (Example 21)

Percussion

D. Burge: *Sources III*
J. Hawkins: *Three Cavatinas*
G. Ligeti: *Nouvelles Aventures*
P. Méfano: *Lignes*
L. de Pablo: *Prosodia*

Keyboard Instruments

W. Albright: *Danse Macabre*
D. Burge: *Sources III*
B. Childs: *Nonet*
S. Lunetta: *Piano Music*
A. Mellnäs: *Tombola*
R. Roxbury: *Aria*
B. Schäffer: *Musica per pianoforte*
E. Schwartz: *Music for Prince Albert*
R. Wilding-White: *Whatzit No. 1*

Strings

B. Childs: *Nonet*
D. Cope: *Angel's Camp II (Example 38); Cedar Breaks*
G. Crumb: *Songs, Drones, and Refrains of Death*
K. Gaburo: *Inside*
G. Heussenstamm: *Pentalogue*
E. Kurtz: *Improvisation for Contrabass*
K. Penderecki: *Capriccio for Violin and Orchestra*

P. Phillips: *Divertimento for Three String Basses*
E. Schwartz: *Music for Prince Albert*

Even more theatrical effects are often demanded in experimental and multimedia works. Percussionists, for example, have been directed to smash bottles or plates of glass (in Ligeti's *Nouvelles Aventures* and William Russell's *Three Dance Movements*, for instance), or to pop inflated balloons with a pin, as in Nicolas Slonimsky's *My Toy Balloon* (see page 183f.). The brass players in *Aura* of Arne Mellnäs must attach balloons to their music stands and explode them with a pin at certain designated moments.

Not primarily a theatrical but rather a sonic device is the "Doppler effect." One cannot deny, however, the visual contribution to any performance moment calling for this gesture. Named after its inventor, Christian Johann Doppler (1803–53), it is accomplished by rotating or pivoting the bell of a brass instrument from one side to the other, or from high to low, with varying speeds and angles of trajectory. The technique can also be applied to the clarinet and saxophone, and rather less successfully to oboe and English horn. (See, for example, Harrison Birtwistle's *Verses for Ensemble* and Philippe Boesman's *Correlations*.)

In addition to the visual stimulation created by this action, an apparent shift in frequencies and in dynamics and/or timbre is produced, owing to the motion of the sound source. The following works request the use of this viable technique:

C. Alsina: *Trio 1967*
D. Burge: *Sources III*
J. Fulkerson: *Patterns III*
I. Xenakis: *Eonta*

The "Doppler effect" has also been used effectively by the horns, alternately stopping and opening the notated pitches at the same time as the instrument bell is pivoted; see Example 23.

Auxiliary Instruments

A final theatricality much in evidence in contemporary scores is the playing upon auxiliary instruments by various instrumentalists (and singers). Generally, the auxiliary instruments are percussion—finger cymbals, woodblocks, a

128

Example 23   Tomasz Sikorski: from *Prologues* (p. 3)

tambourine, pair of maracas, and the like. Frequently, too, wind or string players must perform with mallets or their hands on the interior areas of the piano. These several requirements appear in:

> W. Albright: *Danse Macabre*
> C. Alsina: *Trio 1967*
> I. Anhalt: *Foci*
> D. Burge: *Sources III*
> D. Cope: *Indices*
> B. Johnston: *One Man*
> E. Schwartz: *Options I*
> L. Widdoes: *From a Time of Snow*

In Arne Mellnäs's *Aura* the woodwind and brass players are directed—in addition to popping balloons as previously mentioned—to hang small bottles from their music racks and to strike them with long-handled spoons. And manifestly unconventional auxiliary instruments are the three smoking pipes to be "played" by a flutist, horn player, and trumpeter at the outset of Yizhak Sadai's orchestral *Nuances*—not to mention the slide flutes and assorted bird-calls to be played by all the wind performers in Marius Constant's *Winds*.

Percussionists are now quite frequently instructed to play inside a grand piano, its lid removed, with mallets or other striking agents. Nearly always the player stands at the left side of the piano in order to reach the bass strings with ease. The following scores have required this performance practice:

> Z. Durko: *Iconography No. 2*
> D. Erb: *Concerto for Solo Percussionist; The Seventh Trumpet*
> L. Kirchner: *Music for Orchestra*
> G. Ligeti: *Aventures*
> G. Read: *Haiku Seasons*

In the third book of *Madrigals* of George Crumb, a percussionist is directed to play with mallets on the wire bass strings of the harp; at the same time the harpist plays with both hands on the higher strings. A similar action is required in Crumb's *Songs, Drones, and Refrains of Death* on the open strings of a doublebass. In this composer's *Madrigals—I* the solo bassist fingers certain stipulated pitches while the percussionist plays on the four strings with mallets.

Keyboard players, too, have been asked to perform on auxiliary, ready-to-hand percussion instruments. Those that are easily transportable or that can be comfortably handled while seated at the keyboard are most often designated.

Triangle, woodblock, cowbell or a crotale, for instance, are easily managed by a pianist, who can even play on the keyboard with one hand while shaking or beating upon an auxiliary instrument with the other. A good example of this action is to be found in Udo Kasemet's $\sqrt[5]{5}$.

Two of Ligeti's works call for a harpsichordist to perform also on the strings of an adjacent piano: in *Aventures* he is to use soft timpani sticks, and in *Nouvelles Aventures* he must employ two clothes brushes. The organist in Istvan Anhalt's *Foci* is required at one point in the score to play with mallets in the piano interior.

An obvious auxiliary "instrument" for keyboard players, but one surprisingly seldom requisitioned, is a metronome. In Peter Lewis's solo piano *Sweets,* the pianist must turn it on and off, changing its rate of speed, as directed in the music (Example 24).

Members of the string section are perhaps less frequently expected to perform on auxiliary instruments than other instrumentalists. But in Crumb's *Black Angels* for electrified string quartet the players all must handle various percussion, including bowing on the rim of a tam-tam and on the rims of a set of tuned crystal glasses. These requirements admirably complement the disembodied sounds produced by amplification of the strings in altissimo positions.

No doubt the ultimate in the requirement of auxiliary instruments occurs in *Terretektorh* of Xenakis: each of the eighty-eight orchestral instrumentalists must play, in addition to his own instrument, a woodblock, a whip, a maraca, and a siren whistle. The latter, in three sizes and with three correspondingly different registers, produces "sounds resembling flames," to quote the composer. An additional innovative feature of this work is that the orchestra mem-

Example 24   Peter Lewis: from *Sweets* (p. 4)

For concert performance SWEET 3 requires a metronome, preferably electric, to be placed at the pianist's convenience and "played" as indicated in the score.

bers are to be seated amidst the audience, the performance area thus being integrated with that customarily occupied by the listeners.

Bizarre as many of the extramusical stipulations discussed in this chapter undoubtedly are, they yet form an integral part of the vanguard composer's aesthetic premise. As logical extensions of the concept of "total theatre" the histrionic effects must be assessed within the contexts of the specific compositions requiring them. If not all multimedia works demanding theatrical gestures from their participating instrumentalists are artistically viable, neither are all traditionally conceived and executed works. If some avant-garde musical essays are sophomoric and boring, then so are some earnest and well-meaning pieces in conventional idioms. The efficacy of any one, or all, of these extramusical devices depends not upon their mere presence in today's experimental vocal and instrumental scores but upon the conviction with which they are carried out by the performers involved and by their dramatic impact upon the totality of the musical experience.

Part II

Idiomatic

Techniques

9

WOODWINDS AND BRASSES

Flutter-tonguing Variants

Neither new nor uncommon, the highly favored technique of flutter-tonguing appears in several new guises in vanguard scores. One is to request a gradual and measured shift from normal tonguing to fluttering, or the reverse—though both procedures are easier in theory than in actual practice. Many recent works have requested these tonguing shifts, among them:

N. T. Dao: *Tây Nguyên*
J. Druckman: *Animus 1* (Example 29)
V. Globokar: *Etude pour Folklora II*
D. Kam: *Rendezvous II*
M. Kelemen: *Study for Flute Alone*
B. Schäffer: *Azione a due*
K. Stockhausen: *Momente*
W. Szalonek: *Les Sons*

Flutter-tonguing may also begin suddenly on a sustained note or, conversely, change abruptly into normal single-, double-, or triple-tonguing (as in the *Keime und Male* of Hans-Joachim Hespos). Also, flutter-tonguing, as with other tonguing patterns, may be combined with fingered and valve glissandi:

R. Aitken: *Kebyar*

M. Bamert: *Woodwind Quintet*

M. Ellis: *Mutations* (Example 6)

G. Read: *Sonoric Fantasia No. 3* (Example 25)

G. Schuller: *Spectra*

E. Varèse: *Ameriques*

I. Xenakis: *Eonta*

On oboe and English horn an authentic flutter-tonguing is impossible, but a "faked" variety can be obtained by diminishing the blowing pressure so as to produce a rough and tremulous sound resembling fluttering (see Szalonek's *Les Sons*). In his *Exospheres* Aurelio de la Vega directs the oboist to approximate flutter-tonguing by beating on the lower three keys while blowing the required pitch. And Elliott Carter appends a footnote to an oboe passage in his *8 Etudes and a Fantasy* suggesting alternating normal fingering with pressing down the low B♭-key to achieve an approximation of flutter-tongue.

For an authentic flutter on an approximate pitch, Witold Szalonek asks the flute soloist in his *Concertino* to enclose the mouthpiece tightly with the lips while trilling with the tongue.

It has been pointed out that the ability of wind players to flutter-tongue is more hereditary than acquired, owing to the physical incapacity of some performers to trill with the tongue. When flutter-tonguing is required of such players, they usually substitute a throat "growl," though prolonged use of this device is rather tiring to the throat muscles. At times this latter technique has been explicitly stipulated:

J. Bark, F. Rabe: *Bolos*

L. Berio: *Gesti*

J. Druckman: *Dark Upon the Harp*

D. Martino: *Strata*

D. Reck: *Blues and Screamer*

T. Takemitsu: *Voice*

I. Xenakis: *Linaia—Agon*

Vibrato

Contemporary composers are usually quite specific in designating the complete absence of woodwind vibrato or, contrariwise, an exaggerated vibrato— both for coloristic reasons. Also, uneven or unstable vibratos are frequently requested in current scores: for example, either nonvibrato gradually moving to full normal or overemphasized vibrato, or a more sporadic shift from one condition to another, may be called for. Among the works requiring these various degrees of vibrato production are included:

Chou Wen-chung: *Cursive*
H. W. Henze: *Sinfonia N. 6*
G. Heussenstamm: *Poikilos*
M. Kagel: *Heterophonie*
B. Levy: *Orbs with Flute*
D. Martino: *Concerto for Wind Quintet*
P. Norgård: *Symphony No. 2*
G. Read: *Sonoric Fantasia No. 3*
D. Reck: *Blues and Screamer*
R. Reynolds: *Quick are the Mouths of Earth; Wedge,* and other works
B. Sakač: *Struktur I*
I. Yun: *Images*

More fanciful vibrato requests have been forthcoming from some recent composers: for example, in his *Nonet* Barney Childs calls for a clarinet and bassoon "schmaltzy" vibrato "to sound like a Guy Lombardo saxophone player of the 1920's." In Conrad de Jong's *Contact* the solo trombonist is to produce an exaggerated vibrato "like Tommy Dorsey," while in his *Changes* Larry Austin requires the trombonist to use a "nanny-goat" vibrato—as graphic a request as can be imagined.

Among the brass instruments, the trombone is frequently directed to produce a "slide vibrato," achieved by rapidly maneuvering the slide between positions so that an actual wavering of pitch is perceived—sometimes as much as a major third. The slide vibrato, it should be noted, is most effective in the middle to upper range of the instrument, where the player has more control of the slide. Works specifically requesting slide vibrato include:

R. Aitken: *Kebyar*
C. Alsina: *Consequenza*
R. du Bois: *Music for a Sliding Trombone*
M. Ellis: *Mutations*
W. Kotonski: *Pour quatre*
E. Krenek: *Five Pieces for Trombone and Piano*
I. Xenakis: *Eonta* (Example 20); *Metastaseis*

A different kind of vibrato, one affecting amplitude rather than frequency, is requested in several works of recent composition; it is referred to as a "smorzato" effect in Bruno Bartolozzi's music. On the flute this is achieved by interrupting the blown tone with an excessive velocity of breath, and with lip or jaw rather than diaphragm action; on the reed instruments it is obtained by "squeezing" the reed with gentle movements of the lips. The result in both instances is a slight oscillation of dynamic level, more apparent in the instruments' lower range than in the higher; see the following:

B. Bartolozzi: *Collage; Concertazioni per Oboe,* and other works
D. Rosenboom: *and come up dripping*
L. Widdoes: *From a Time of Snow*

Fingering devices

Many new woodwind and brass effects relate primarily to fingering patterns or valve combinations rather than to embouchure or breath control. Possibly the most common of these is the single-pitch trill or "timbral tremolo," achieved by rapidly alternating the normal and the harmonic (or other alternative) fingering of the notated, unchanging pitch. Also referred to variously as an enharmonic trill, a "color trill", a unison tremolo, a key vibrato, and "bariolage" (from the string instrument technique of alternating an open string with a fingered note on the same pitch), the technique of alternate fingerings is most frequently demanded of flute and alto flute players. It is less often required of oboists, clarinetists, bassoonists, and saxophonists. The following works all require the application of enharmonic trills from various woodwind instruments:

R. Aitken: *Kebyar*
G. Amy: *Jeux*
T. Antoniou: *Five Likes*
L. Bassett: *Music for Saxophone and Piano*
L. Berio: *Sequenza VII*
J. van de Booren: *Chanson de Printemps*
G. Braun: *Monologe I*
E. Carter: *Sonata for Flute, Oboe, Cello and Harpsichord*
N. Castiglioni: *Alef*
Chou Wen-chung: *Cursive*
G. Crumb: *Eleven Echoes of Autumn* (Example 30); *Madrigals—II*

E. Denisov: *Romantische Musik*

W. Eisma: *World Within World*

D. Erb: *Concerto for Solo Percussionist*

L. Foss: *Echoi*

A. Gilbert: *The Incredible Flute Music*

V. Globokar: *Accord; Discours II*

S. Hodkinson: *Interplay*

K. Huber: *Alveare vernat*

M. Kelemen: *Equilibres*

Example 25   Gardner Read: from *Sonoric Fantasia No. 3* (p. 25)

K. Korte: *Remembrances*

T. de Kruyf: *Mosaico*

K. Penderecki: *Capriccio per Oboe*

G. Read: *Sonoric Fantasia No. 3* (Example 25)

G. Schuller: *Seven Studies on Themes of Paul Klee*

T. Takemitsu: *Eucalypts(I), II*

L. Widdoes: *From a Time of Snow*

A. Woodbury: *Remembrances*

C. Wuorinen: *Flute Variations*

According to that authority on wind instrument techniques, Bruno Barto-lozzi,[1] there are nearly 100 possible fingerings which would produce b[1] on the oboe, thus enabling the player to create a seemingly unending succession of subtle timbral changes on a single pitch. Not all the available notes on the oboe, nor on the other woodwinds, possess so many fingering alternates, but most wind players have not yet fully explored the impressive potential of this viable technique.

Notationally, the standard trill-symbol supplemented by a small zero-sign (tr°) can be used for enharmonic trills (as shown in Example 25) though many composers favor writing out the series of repeated pitches and alternating an N (for normal fingering) and a ° over the note-heads.

On the brass instruments, with the exception of trombone, the enharmonic trill is achieved by an alternation of different valve actions and minute embouchure adjustments (as in Schuller's *Five Pieces for Five Horns*). The trombone, of course, must rely on quick changes of slide position in conjunction with slight changes of embouchure. Examples of brass "bariolage" include:

L. Berio: *Sinfonia*

J. Druckman: *Animus 1*

D. Erb: *Symphony of Overtures*

V. Globokar: *Accord; Etude pour Folklora II,* and other works

A. Imbrie: *Three Sketches for Trombone and Piano*

E. Krenek: *Five Pieces for Trombone and Piano*

D. Reck: *Five Studies for Tuba Alone*

M. Stibilj: *Condensation*

Half-valving (on horn, trumpet, and tuba) is another fingering device in current use; the brass player gradually pushes down the valves half-way, an

---

[1] *New Sounds for Woodwind.*

action that subtly but perceptibly changes both the blown pitch and its timbre (as requested in Ton de Leeuw's *Spatial Music III,* for example). It is an ideal way to "dirty up" a tone, and is highly favored by composers of jazz and rock music.

Another modern fingering device on woodwind and brass instruments is the double trill; it is achieved by rapidly alternating two fingers on a single key or valve of the instrument. The pitch produced is a unison but is slightly "broken" in effect (see Robert Aitken's *Kebyar* and Anthony Gilbert's *The Incredible Flute Music,* for instance).

Breath and Air Sounds

Just as late twentieth-century music exploits the percussive potential of wind instruments, so it has come to explore breath and air effects unrelated to normal tone production. For breath or wind sound alone on an instrument, the player contracts or relaxes his diaphragm without tonguing into mouthpiece or reed. The sounds are achieved by exaggerated emphasis of inhalant or exhalant effort, but without precise embouchure control or fingerings of specific pitches.

On the single- and double-reed instruments the player directs the air stream into the mouthpiece or reed; on members of the flute family the player slightly turns or rolls the instrument away from the lips while blowing air across the mouthpiece opening. This kind of effect was first specified in Heitor Villa-Lobos' *The Jet-Whistle* of 1953: the flutist is directed to close the blowhole tightly with the mouth and to blow violently while fingering low B; the result is a forceful downward "swoosh," without pitch. The same general effect is called for in Sydney Hodkinson's *Interplay* (which he characterizes as a "shriek"), as well as in Donald Erb's *Concerto for Solo Percussionist* and in Harley Gaber's *Voce II.*

A few composers have been unusually graphic in their instructions for wind instrument breath sounds: "Blow sharply into any tone hole [of bassoon] as if to clean it" is the way Barney Childs put it in his *Nonet,* while "Sound produced by sucking" is David Rosenboom's phraseology in *and come up dripping.* In Edward Bogusławski's *Canti* the flutist is told to produce a breath sound "by holding the instrument 1½ cm from the lower lip," while directing the air stream toward the mouthpiece, and in Larry Austin's *Changes* the solo trombonist is instructed to "blow a stream of 'whistling' air" through the instrument.

Other recent scores that require woodwind breath sounds independent of any tone production include:

T. Antoniou: *Five Likes*

E. Brown: *Available Forms 2; Times Five,* and other works

T. Bruynel: *Signs*

N. Castiglioni: *Consonante*

F. Cerha: *Enjambments*

S. Cervetti: *Six Sequences*

B. Childs: *Nonet*

G. Crumb: *Echoes of Time and the River; Eleven Echoes of Autumn,* and other works

N. T. Dao: *Tây Nguyên*

W. Eisma: *Non-lecture II*

D. Erb: *The Seventh Trumpet*

L. Ferrari: *Société II*

L. Foss: *Orpheus*

H. Gaber: *Voce II*

V. Globokar: *Accord*

C. Halffter: *Lineas y puntos; Planto por las victimas de la violencia*

H-J. Hespos: *Passagen*

S. Hodkinson: *Fresco*

J. Ibert: *Suite Symphonique*

M. Kelemen: *Entrances*

B. Levy: *Orbs with Flute*

G. Ligeti: *Apparitions; Aventures,* and other works

R. Maros: *Eufonia No. 3*

D. Martino: *Concerto for Wind Quintet*

T. Mayuzumi: *Metamusic*

R. Meale: *Clouds now and then*

J. Mekeel: *The Shape of Silence*

F. Miroglio: *Phases; Réfractions*

P. Norgård: *Symphony No. 2*

B. Rands: *Actions for six; Ballad I,* and other works

M. Subotnick: *Lamination I*

W. Szalonek: *Aarhus Music*

A. de la Vega: *Interpolation for Solo Clarinet*

B. A. Zimmermann: *Tempus loquendi*

Similar directives for the brass instruments, individually or collectively, are to be found in the following scores:

C. Alsina: *Trio 1967* (Example 22)

L. Austin: *Changes*

M. Bamert: *Inkblot*

J. Bark, F. Rabe: *Bolos*

D. Bedford: *Trona*

E. Brown: *Available Forms 2; From Here*

S. Bussotti; *Torso*

G. Cacioppo: *Time on Time in Miracles*

J. Cage: *Solo for Sliding Trombone*

B. Childs: *Music for Trombone*

M. Colgrass: *As Quiet As*

G. Crumb: *Echoes of Time and the River*

N. T. Dao: *Phū-Dông*

J. Druckman: *Animus 1* (Example 29)

D. Erb: *Concerto for Solo Percussionist; Symphony of Overtures,* and other works

L. Ferrari: *Société II*

L. Foss: *For 24 Winds*

V. Globokar: *Etude pour Folklora II*

C. Halffter: *Lineas y puntos; Planto por las victimas de la violencia*

R. Haubenstock-Ramati: *Credentials*

W. Heider: *-einander*

H. W. Henze: *Sinfonia N. 6*

S. Hodkinson: *Fresco*

A. Lanza: *Acúfenos I*

G. Ligeti: *Aventures; Nouvelles Aventures,* and other works

R. Maros: *Eufonia No. 3*

R. Meale: *Clouds now and then*

A. Mellnäs: *Gestes sonores*

M. Mitrea-Celarianu: *Seth*

W. Ross: *Concerto for Trombone*

W. Sydeman: *Texture Studies*

An instrumental simulation of electronic "white noise" is requested by James Fulkerson in *Patterns III*, the solo tuba player being directed to blow air into the mouthpiece through clenched teeth. In Nguyen Thien Dao's *Phū-Dông*, on the other hand, the player is to "suck in air through the mouthpiece like a kiss"; also to blow into the bell of the instrument—the latter an awkward requirement to ask of any tuba performer.

A trill or tremolo effect with the breath alone (but into the instrument) is the rough equivalent of flutter-tonguing without tone; it has been demanded in the following works:

W. Albright: *Danse Macabre*
J. Bark, F. Rabe: *Bolos*
L. Berio: *Gesti*
G. Braun: *Monologe I*
S. Bussotti: *Couple; Torso*
S. Cervetti; *Six Sequences*
A. Corghi: *Stereofonie X4*
G. Crumb: *Eleven Echoes of Autumn*
L. Ferrari: *Société II*
V. Globokar: *Discours II*
G. Ligeti: *Ten Pieces for Wind Quintet*
M. Mitrea-Celarianu: *Seth*
P. Norgård: *Prism*
E. Schwartz: *Options I*
A. de la Vega: *Interpolation for Solo Clarinet*
D. Wilson: *Doubles*

In his composition cited, Cervetti directs the brass players to flutter-tongue into the instrument with the mouthpiece removed, an effect virtually indistinguishable from an unpitched breath tremolo.

Breath sounds may also be combined with actual instrumental tone, emphasizing the one or the other in varying degrees; see:

W. Albright: *Danse Macabre*
G. Braun: *Monologe I*
G. Crumb: *Eleven Echoes of Autumn* (Example 30)
V. Globokar: *Discours II*
D. Martino: *Concerto for Wind Quintet*
L. Widdoes: *From a Time of Snow*

In addition, percussive devices (key or valve clicks, or audible fingerings) may be freely mixed with unpitched air sounds, as found, for instance, in these scores:

T. Albert: *Sound Frames*
W. Albright: *Danse Macabre*
F. Cerha: *Enjambments*
H-J. Hespos: *Passagen*
B. Jolas: *Fusain*
B. Maderna: *Concerto for Oboe*

R. Moryl: *Improvisations*
M. Subotnick: *Lamination I*

Most commonly used in the production of harmonics (see pages 52–54), the technique of overblowing has been stipulated by several composers in their wind parts to alter pitch and timbre, such as breath sound to clear tone, or the reverse (as in the *Keime und Male* of Hespos). Overblowing has been specified to achieve a harsh and strained tonal quality (in Paul Chihara's *Branches*, for example), and to produce a shrill wind sound (Crumb's *Eleven Echoes of Autumn*).

The wind instruments are all capable of producing attacks that emphasize a strong breathy quality. In Marc Wilkinson's *Voices* the composer asks for a "soft, windy attack"; later, one articulated by the player pronouncing "the," and at still another point, a sharp attack with an exaggerated "t" sound. There are similar directives to the wind players in the *Bolos* of Bark and Rabe, John Cage's *Solo for Sliding Trombone*, and *Interpolation* of Aurelio de la Vega.

Both the woodwinds and the brasses can articulate into the instrument mouthpiece without producing a specific pitch; this special effect has been specified in David Bedford's *Trona*, Ernst Krenek's *Five Pieces for Trombone and Piano*, and Ligeti's *Apparitions*, among other works. Somewhat related to this effect are "ghost notes," which are staples of jazz performance. They are pitches blown so softly that they are almost inaudible. In Gunther Schuller's words, "a 'ghost note' is sort of 'swallowed' by the player, giving it almost no air support and no projection." Examination of Schuller's *Journey into Jazz* will show this technique at work.

In proportionately notated music (time-notation) wind players are frequently instructed to hold a tone until their breath is exhausted. To do so produces a noticeable decay of both amplitude and frequency. See, for instance:

D. Bedford: *Music for Albion Moonlight*
A. Gilbert: *The Incredible Flute Music*
J. Heinke: *Music for Trombone and Percussion*
G. Ligeti: *Aventures*
P. Méfano: *Paraboles*
F. Miroglio: *Phases; Réfractions*
T. Takemitsu: *Eucalypts (I)*

In both *Aarhus Music* and *Les Sons*, Witold Szalonek directs the flutist to blow normally, to the opposite side of the mouthpiece, but to change the angle of airflow by turning the instrument in such a way that a full tone is not obtained.

Bernard Rands asks for similar action on the flutist's part in his *Actions for six*. Werner Heider includes directions in his solo recorder *Katalog* to produce a breathy, exhalant effect, and to create the sound of rushing air on a definite pitch with perceptible but rather weak overtones.

Mention must be made of "beat [or beating] tones," achieved either by a single wind instrument playing intervallic structures or by two instruments of similar timbre playing together. As a concrete example of the first category: in Lukas Foss's wind quintet (*Cave of the Winds*) the four woodwinds are each directed to hold certain blown pitches, gradually increasing both air and lip pressure; the result is a microtonal multiphonic whose composite tones create amplitude beats at regularly recurring intervals.

In the second symphony of Per Norgård, amplitude beats are to be produced by two clarinets playing soft pitches a microtone apart. And as a dedicated advocate of this acoustical device, Iannis Xenakis calls for beating tones between clarinet and cello in *Charisma* and between horn and trombone in *Linaia—Agon;* in each instance the composer indicates a fluctuating number of amplitude beats per second. Thus, in these and other recent vanguard works, an acoustical phenomenon once accidentally created by faulty intonation is now an actively sought after sonic effect by our experimentally motivated composers.

Mouthpiece and Tubing Effects

A technical phenomenon of recent vintage, one congenital to both woodwind and brass instruments, is the production of sound or indefinite noise on the reed or mouthpiece alone, removed from the instrument. Obviously, no precise pitches are heard when the player blows on these agents unattached to his instrument, but an illusion of relative pitch (high, medium, low) can be obtained through embouchure manipulation.

Various vanguard composers have asked the double-reed players to "crow" on the detached reed, producing a harsh squawk:

T. Bruynel: *Signs*
B. Childs: *Nonet*
D. Erb: *Concerto for Solo Percussionist*
R. Felciano: *Contractions*
S. Hodkinson: *Fresco*
A. Hrisanide: *A la recherche de la verticale*
D. Rosenboom: *and come up dripping*
A. de la Vega: *Exospheres for Oboe and Piano*

Actually, two kinds of sound can be obtained by this action: open, the reed held in the fingers while enclosed with the lips; muted, the other hand cupped around the reed to muffle the sound.

It is possible to make a transition from an unpitched squawk on the reed to a fully pitched tone by gradually pushing the staple back into the instrument while blowing; this directive to the player appears in David Cope's *Indices* for solo oboe.

Composers of experimental music also frequently direct the woodwind players to blow into the instrument after removing the mouthpiece or reed. Flutists are instructed to blow into the detached head-joint or else into the barrel itself, as required by Barney Childs in *Jack's New Bag,* Matthias Bamert in *Inkblot,* and David Bedford in *Trona.* It is also possible to play into the body of the instrument, the head-joint removed, with an oboe, clarinet, or bassoon reed, or with various brass mouthpieces. Of these various unconventional agents, however, only a clarinet or bassoon reed produces a viable sound effect.

Reed instrument players have been frequently asked to take the reeds completely out of the staple or mouthpiece and to blow directly into the tube opening, as in:

H. Holliger: *Siebengesang*
G. Ligeti: *Apparitions; Ten Pieces for Wind Quintet*
Y. Yannay: *preFIX-FIX-sufFIX*

The oboist in *Jack's New Bag* is also directed to reverse his instrument and to blow forcefully into the bell. And both Childs in his *Nonet* and William Sydeman in *Texture Studies* request the bassoonist in their works to remove the reed from the mouthpiece and to tongue into either the neck or the crook of the instrument. Other recent composers have asked that the woodwind and brass players blow forcibly (like a "phh") into the tubing, with the reed or mouthpiece out:

B. Childs: *Jack's New Bag*
M. Constant: *Winds*
A. Hrisanide: *A la recherche de la verticale*
M. Kelemen: *Entrances*
G. Ligeti: *Apparitions*

Among a number of other avant-garde scores that require mouthpiece or reed effects, independent of the instrument, we might cite:

T. Antoniou: *Five Likes*
D. Bedford: *Gastrula: That White and Radiant Legend*
A. Bloch: *Erwartung*
B. Childs: *Nonet*
M. Ellis: *Mutations*
D. Erb: The Seventh Trumpet; Symphony of Overtures
L. Ferrari: *Société II*
C. Halffter: *Anillos*
H. W. Henze: *Sinfonia N. 6*
W. Kilar: *Générique*
A. Mellnäs: *Aura*
K. Penderecki: *Fluorescences*
Z. Rudzinski: *Contra Fidem*
B. Sakač: *Struktur I*
B. Schäffer: *Scultura*
M. Subotnick: *Lamination I*
W. Szalonek: *Concertino per flauto; Les Sons*
R. Wittinger: *Om*

In addition to the foregoing, several other unusual mouthpiece effects have been stipulated by vanguardists in their scores:

1. Speaking words over the flute mouthpiece ("speak-flute") while fingering certain notated pitches

   G. Crumb: *Madrigals—IV*

2. Forcibly blowing a "swoosh" into the detached mouthpiece

   S. Cervetti: *Six Sequences*
   B. Childs: *Jack's New Bag*
   P. Méfano: *Lignes*

3. Making a kind of "fore-sound" by blowing a broad air-stream at the mouthpiece from a short distance

   W. Kilar: *Générique*

4. "Kissing" with the lips against the detached mouthpiece, which produces a sharp, non-pitched and accented sound

   M. Bamert: *Inkblot*
   S. Hodkinson: *Fresco*

5. Making a squeaky sound by sucking with the lips on the mouthpiece

    R. Aitken: *Kebyar*
    L. Austin: *Changes*
    B. Childs: *Music for Trombone*
    D. Rosenboom: *and come up dripping*

6. Making a high-pitched whistle through the mouthpiece

    J. Fulkerson: *Patterns III*

7. Whistling over the stem of the brass mouthpiece, the hand covering the other end

    E. Krenek: *Five Pieces for Trombone and Piano*

8. "Buzzing" into a detached brass instrument mouthpiece, either open or closed, the latter effect achieved by cupping the hand over the mouthpiece

    L. Austin: *Changes*
    J. Bark, F. Rabe: *Bolos*
    D. Erb: *Concerto for Solo Percussionist; The Seventh Trumpet*
    S. Hodkinson: *Fresco*
    A. Lanza: *Eidesis II*

9. Blowing into the horn with inverted mouthpiece

    Y. Yannay: *preFIX-FIX-sufFIX*

Trombonists are sometimes directed to blow or buzz through the detached slide (Barney Childs so requests in *Jack's New Bag*). Also, they must sometimes make audible inhalant and exhalant noises with the moist lips into the mouthpiece, independent of tone production:

    C. Alsina: *Consecuenza; Trio 1967*
    L. Berio: *Sequenza V*
    J. Druckman: *Animus 1*
    V. Globokar: *Discours II*
    M. Stibilj: *Condensation*

In Roger Reynolds' *Blind Men*, the trombonist is asked to produce high, whistlelike sounds by using a trumpet (smaller bore) mouthpiece; in *Patterns III*, James Fulkerson requests similar sounds, but does not specify a change of mouthpiece.

Other possibilities for unconventional sound production on the trombone, the most favored of the brasses among the avant-garde, include removing either the outer slide, the tuning slide, or the F-attachment slide and blowing into the instrument, with or without mouthpiece. See, for example:

> L. Austin: *Changes*
> J. Cage: *Solo for Sliding Trombone*
> E. Krenek: *Five Pieces for Trombone and Piano*

An intriguing "echo" effect can be obtained by taking out the F-attachment, blowing a pitch and, at the same time, flipping on the F-attachment lever; the result is a double sound—from the bell and from the open tube at the rear of the instrument. This device appears in the Krenek work cited above.

Multiphonics

Of all the newer techniques applicable to the wind instruments, none figure more prominently in the scores of the avant-garde than multiphonics. The result of certain combinations of embouchure, unusual fingerings, and auxiliary keys or valves, multiphonics create sounds that extend from a simple interval of two pitches to complex chords of four, five, or six notes.[2] Thus, instruments that have long been considered as strictly unisonal have been liberated to the extent that they can now produce harmonic structures, though admittedly the individual tones vary considerably in amplitude and timbre, not to say in certainty of production.

Multiphonic chords are composed, in reality, of a blown fundamental plus certain harmonics of theoretically equal amplitude. Such structures can be completely homogeneous in timbre, but they may be heterogeneous as well, each note in the structure having a subtly different coloring. These chords result from fingering patterns that in principle provide several tube-lengths on which to produce composite tones. Double harmonics, as well as microtonal inflections, can be incorporated into multiphonic chords, and multiple trills can often be created between two such multipitched structures. Parenthetically, it may be noted that all varieties of tonguing, including flutter-tongue, may be applied to most multiphonics, though usually at a low level of intensity. No multiphonic structures, however, can utilize vibrato, as the air flow must be stable to produce such chords.

All of the standard woodwinds can produce multiphonics, though the com-

---

[2] According to Robert Dick (see Bibliography), every known flute fingering can produce at least one multiple sonority, and more commonly from four to six such structures. At least 1,000 flute multiphonics have so far been catalogued.

plexity of the structures, the ease with which they are produced, and the relative quality of sound vary considerably from instrument to instrument. The majority of the examples found in recent scores relate to the four regulars—flute, oboe, clarinet, and bassoon. Fewer instances of multiphonic structures for piccolo, alto flute, English horn, bass clarinet (see Henze's *Heliogabalus Imperator*), saxophone, and contrabassoon are to be located in new compositions; this imbalance may in time change as the technique itself is more thoroughly developed and refined for all the instruments of the section.

The concept of multiphonics also includes sung and hummed pitches superimposed on blown tones. That is, the wind player is asked to sing or hum either the same pitch he is blowing or a different note, thus creating a simple two-voiced polyphony with two distinct timbres. The brass instruments as well as the woodwinds are capable of utilizing this technique; indeed, multiphonics for the brasses are limited to this type of multiple-tone production and thus to two-note structures only. Owing to the basic construction and the sound-producing principle of the instruments, the brasses cannot create the more complex sonorities generally available to the woodwinds. Although a "difference tone" is theoretically present when a blown brass note is coupled with a sung or hummed pitch a tenth higher, it is so faint as to be virtually inaudible.

A composer may direct in his score that either the vocalizations or the blown tones gain the ascendant; that is, the player may gradually stop sounding various pitches and end by only singing or humming, or he may accomplish the direct reverse. Either or both of these stipulations are to be found in:

L. Berio: *Gesti*
A. Gilbert: *The Incredible Flute Music*
V. Globokar: *Discours II*
B. Jolas: *Fusain*
J. Mekeel: *The Shape of Silence*

The sung or hummed pitch may also waver above or below a lipped pitch after beginning in unison, or it may contract into a unison after commencing at a certain interval from the blown pitch (as in David Cope's *Indices* and James Heinke's *Music for Trombone and Percussion*).

The problem of accurately notating multiphonics is twofold: first, the composer must know what structures are possible on the various wind instruments and, second, he must know how to indicate clearly the required fingering patterns. Generally speaking, these notations should conform to the diagrams shown in Examples 2 and 26, included either in prefatory notes to the composition or else placed above or below the staff at the appropriate moments.

Example 26   Claire Polin: from *The Death of Procris* (p. 1)

Curiously, multiphonic chords for various of the woodwinds in Harrison Birtwistle's *Verses for Ensemble* are notated on three staves each. The reason— and necessity—for this visual complexity is not clear.

Additional technical expertise, both as to possible structures and to their notations, is available in the following reference sources:

Bruno Bartolozzi: *New Sounds for Woodwind*
Robert Dick: *The Other Flute*
John Heiss: *Some Multiple Sonorities for Flute, Oboe, Clarinet, and Bassoon*
Thomas Howell: *The Avant-Garde Flute*
James Pellerite: *A Modern Guide to Fingerings for the Flute*[3]

There is one further problem for the notator of multiphonics that include hummed or sung pitches, albeit a minor one: to be realistic, two vocal pitches ought to be indicated, one for a high (or female) voice and another at the lower octave for a low (male) voice. This is no token gesture to Women's Liberation but is a matter of compositional accuracy; the register relationship of the vocal to the blown tones will naturally vary according to the gender of the performer.

Among the innumerable recent compositions that feature multiphonics, in addition to those previously mentioned, are included:

Piccolo, flute, and/or alto flute

B. Bartolozzi: *Concertazioni a quattro; Tres Recuerdos del cielo,* and other works
L. Berio: *Sequenza I*

---

[3] Refer to Bibliography for details concerning these sources.

R. S. Brindle: *Andromeda M. 31*

T. Bruynel: *Signs*

Chou Wen-chung: *Cursive*

L. Foss: *Cave of the Winds*

K. Gaburo: *Two*

J. Heiss: *Movements for Three Flutes*

H. W. Henze: *Heliogabalus Imperator*

B. Levy: *Orbs with Flute*

G. Ligeti: *Aventures*

C. Polin: *The Death of Procris.* (Example 26); *O, Aderyn Pur*

R. Reynolds: *Quick are the Mouths of Earth* (Example 27); *Traces,* and other works

W. Szalonek: *Aarhus Music; Proporzioni II,* and other works

T. Takemitsu: *Eucalypts (I); Voice,* and other works

L. Widdoes: *From a Time of Snow*

B. A. Zimmermann: *Tempus loquendi*

Recorder

W. Heider: *Katalog*

Oboe and/or English horn

T. Albert: *Sound Frames*

G. Amy: *Jeux*

T. Antoniou: *Five Likes*

B. Bartolozzi: *Collage; Concertazioni per Oboe,* and other works

L. Berio: *Sequenza VII*

E. Denisov: *Romantische Musik*

D. Erb: *Symphony of Overtures*

L. Foss: *Orpheus*

V. Globokar: *Discours III*

H. W. Henze: *Heliogabalus Imperator*

T. de Kruyf: *Mosaico*

K. Penderecki: *Capriccio per Oboe*

D. Rosenboom: *and come up dripping*

W. Szalonek: *Aarhus Music* (Example 28)

T. Takemitsu: *Eucalypts (I), II*

Clarinet and/or bass clarinet

R. Aitken: *Kebyar*

B. Bartolozzi: *Concertazioni a quattro; Tres Recuerdos del cielo*

P. M. Davies: *Eight Songs for a Mad King*

D. Erb: *Symphony of Overtures*

Example 27   Roger Reynolds: from *Quick are the Mouths of Earth* (p. 4)

L. Foss: *Cave of the Winds*
H. W. Henze: *Heliogabalus Imperator*
R. Reynolds: *I/O*
W. Szalonek: *Aarhus Music* (Example 28)
A. de la Vega: *Interpolation for Solo Clarinet*
D. Wilson: *Doubles*

Bassoon and/or contrabassoon

B. Bartolozzi: *Concertazioni a quattro; Tres Recuerdos del cielo*
D. Erb: *Symphony of Overtures*
L. Foss: *Cave of the Winds*
H. W. Henze: *Heliogabalus Imperator*
W. Szalonek: *Aarhus Music* (Example 28)
D. Wilson: *Doubles*
Y. Yannay: *preFIX-FIX-sufFIX*

Saxophone

W. Duckworth: *Reel Music*
C. Polin: *O, Aderyn Pur*

Works calling for brass instrument multiphonics, limited to simultaneous vocalized and blown pitches, include:

Horn

G. Cacioppo: *Time on Time in Miracles*
G. Ligeti: *Aventures; Nouvelles Aventures*
K. Stockhausen: *Adieu*
Y. Yannay: *preFIX-FIX-sufFIX*

Trumpet

B. Childs: *Nonet*

Trombone

R. Aitken: *Kebyar*
C. Alsina: *Consequenza; Trio 1967*
L. Austin: *Changes*
J. Bark, F. Rabe: *Bolos*
L. Berio: *Sequenza V*
R. du Bois: *Music for a Sliding Trombone*
G. Cacioppo: *Time on Time in Miracles*
B. Childs: *Music for Trombone*

Example 28   Witold Szalonek: from *Aarhus Music* (p. 7)

156

J. Druckman: *Animus 1* (Example 29)

R. Erickson: *Ricercar à 5*

J. Fulkerson: *Patterns III*

V. Globokar: *Accord*

A. Imbrie: *Three Sketches for Trombone and Piano*

E. Krenek: *Five Pieces for Trombone and Piano*

K. Kroeger: *Toccata for Clarinet, Trombone and Percussion*

B. Rands: *Ballad I*

E. Schwartz: *Options I; Rip*

Tuba

C. Polin: *The Death of Procris*

D. Reck: *Five Studies for Tuba Alone*

Vocalizations

Vocal effects other than singing and humming—speaking, whispering, laughing, enunciating vowels and consonants, and the like, and combined with the production of specific pitches—are rapidly becoming equally standard multiphonic procedures. In his *Music for Trombone,* for instance, Barney Childs directs the player to "mutter, talk, yell—all manner of rhythmically irregular violent vocal sounds while playing a sustained pitch." And not to be outdone, Robert Erickson in *Ricercar à 5* tells the trombonist to "bellow in imitation of cows" while playing. Equally theatrical is Donald Erb's directive in *The Seventh Trumpet*: "Almost all the wind players shout and scream angry things through their instruments. This gradually diminishes to a mutter, then to a whisper."

The following list is a sampling of recent compositions that call for such vocalizations from wind players:

W. Albright: *Danse Macabre*

M. Bamert: *Inkblot*

L. Berio: *Sequenza V*

E. Brown: *Available Forms 2; Hodograph I,* and other works

P. Chihara: *Willow, Willow*

B. Childs: *Jack's New Bag; Nonet,* and other works

G. Crumb: *Echoes of Time and the River*

J. Druckman: *Animus 1* (Example 29)

H. Gaber: *Voce II*

V. Globokar: *Accord; Discours II,* and other works

Example 29   Jacob Druckman: from *Animus 1* (p. 5)

Indicates pitches to be sung while playing. As the vocal note passes a unison, or other perfect interval, amplitude modulation (beats), will occur.

Indicates non-vocalized sounds (loud whispers), to be articulated into the trombone. International Phonetic Alphabet symbols used are: **tʃə** as in CHUnk, **kə** as in CAreen, **x** as in German aCH.

Indicates non-voiced forming of the diphthong to change timbre of the played note.

Indicates a loud, implosive clicking of the tongue into the trombone, (similar to the white noise sounds on the tape).

Indicates air to be blown into the mouthpiece with no lip vibration, the air stream to be cut sharply by the tongue against the lips, producing a hint of the pedal tone.

Play through once, continue to play groups separated by rests in any order until end of time span indicated by length of box.

Plunger opened and closed as rapidly as possible, but not coordinated with double tonguing. Tonguing will proceed more rapidly than plunger.

Bell half-covered by plunger.

Begin fluttertongue gradually.

W. Heider: *-einander; Katalog*

J. Heinke: *Music for Trombone and Percussion*

H-J. Hespos: *Passagen*

S. Hodkinson: *Interplay*

M. Kagel: *Anagrama*

G. Ligeti: *Aventures; Nouvelles Aventures,* and other works

J. Mekeel: *The Shape of Silence*

M. Mitrea-Celarianu: *Seth*

B. Rands: *Ballad I*

R. Reynolds: *Ambages; Blind Men,* and other works

W. Szalonek: *Aarhus Music*

T. Takemitsu: *Voice*

E. Varèse: *Ameriques*

A. de la Vega: *Interpolation for Solo Clarinet*

Nonvocalized sounds (mutterings, barks, hisses, grunts, yelps, coughs, buzzes, groans, and assorted squawks) may be combined with fingered pitches on both woodwind and brass instruments; they may also be articulated through the instrument without fingering specific pitches. Among a number of recent works calling for these effects one might mention:

C. Alsina: *Trio 1967*

J. Bark, F. Rabe: *Bolos*

J. Cage: *Solo for Sliding Trombone*

G. Crumb: *Echoes of Time and the River*

J. Druckman: *Animus 1* (Example 29)

D. Erb: *Concerto for Solo Percussionist*

V. Globokar: *Accord; Discours II,* and other works

G. Heussenstamm: *Poikilos*

E. Krenek: *Five Pieces for Trombone and Piano*

B. Rands: *Ballad I*

D. Reck: *Blues and Screamer*

W. Szalonek: *Aarhus Music*

Speech sounds or other vocalizations, including singing and humming, and noises may be directed into the mouthpiece alone, taken from the instrument. These requirements may be found in the following scores:

J. Bark, F. Rabe: *Bolos*

L. Berio: *Sequenza V*

P. Chihara: *Willow, Willow*
J. Druckman: *Animus 1* (Example 29)
J. Fulkerson: *Patterns III*
V. Globokar: *Accord*
M. Mitrea-Celarianu: *Seth*
D. Reck: *Five Studies for Tuba Alone*
R. Wittinger: *Om*

Miscellaneous Effects

Several recent wind-instrument effects capitalize on the principle of sympathetic vibration: one is the "Duffalo effect," invented by Richard Duffalo, an original member of Lukas Foss's improvisation group. The device, which Foss first used in *Echoi,* consists of the clarinetist's gently moving the bell of his instrument over the head of one timpano while blowing specific pitches, the angle and speed of movement ad libitum. The drumhead acts as a resonator, picking up the vibrations of the clarinet sound and subtly altering its pitch and timbre as the instrument bell moves freely over the membrane. The identical action is required of the solo trombonist in the *Dialogues* of Dennis Good.

A related sonic effect is obtained by a wind player's directing his playing into the interior of a grand piano, the sustaining pedal held down by the pianist, or—as in the case of David Cope's solo oboe *Indices*—depressed by mechanical means, such as a heavy brick. Other works that call for this effect are:

D. Bedford: *Music for Albion Moonlight*
G. Crumb: *Eleven Echoes of Autumn* (Example 30)
R. L. Finney: *Divertissement*
L. Foss: *Echoi*
P. Patterson: *Rebecca*

This device is most feasible, of course, for the flute and oboe family members and for the clarinet; it would be more difficult, not to say impractical, for bass clarinet, saxophone, bassoon and contrabassoon.

Singly or in ensemble, the brasses have also been directed to blow pitches into the interior of the piano—a device widely favored at one time in the big jazz bands. The following vanguard works require this procedure:

A. Imbrie: *Three Sketches for Trombone and Piano*
E. Krenek: *Five Pieces for Trombone and Piano*

Example 30 George Crumb: from *Eleven Echoes of Autumn* (p. 9)

E. Schwartz: *Music for Napoleon and Beethoven* (Example 21); *Options I*
I. Xenakis: *Eonta*

Raising the bell of a brass instrument on high to achieve a measure of added volume is not, of course, a new device in orchestration. In Henze's virtuoso *Heliogabalus Imperator,* however, the four trumpeters are directed to gradually raise their instrument bells while sustaining a high pitch. The result, visual as well as acoustic, can be described as a modified version of the "Doppler effect" (see page 127).

Hybrid Instruments

During the present century no patently new instruments have been added to the existing families of the woodwinds and brasses. To counterbalance this lack of new instrumental sound resource, today's orchestrators are experimenting with hybrid instruments. Attaching woodwind reeds to a brass instrument tubing, or using a brass mouthpiece on a woodwind barrel are two ways of creating "new" instruments. Also, a certain amount of intra-choir exchange of sound-producing apparatus may take place. For example: the flute tubing (with head-joint removed) may be played upon with oboe, bassoon, or clarinet reed; the oboe or English horn may substitute a bassoon reed for their customary equipment, while a bassoonist may produce his sounds with an oboe reed.

Likewise, the different brass instruments may exchange mouthpieces, the horn functioning with a trombone mouthpiece, for instance, or the trumpet using a tuba mouthpiece. Obviously, the utilization of a large-bore mouthpiece on a relatively small tubing, or a small-bore mouthpiece on an instrument having a larger tubing presents problems of embouchure. Although the sonic results of these experimentations are intriguing and, to a considerable extent, viable, there is no uniformity in quality or predictable new timbre so produced. The interested composer is urged to probe further in the area of hybrid instruments, ideally in collaboration with experienced and highly capable performers.

Bruno Bartolozzi has stated (in *New Sounds for Woodwind*) a truism that bears repetition: "The evolution of instrumental music has always been brought about by reciprocal collaboration between composers and performers . . . That composers and performers have sometimes in the past been one and the same person does not alter the problem in the least . . . The fact remains that true instrumental conquests have never been the fruit of abstract conceptions, but of toilsome direct experience." This statement indubitably applies to the totality of techniques discussed throughout this book, whether they are of traditional lineage or are manifestly new in concept. There is no reason to believe that the historic process will change in the years to come.

10

PERCUSSION

Tuning of Unpitched Instruments

Until the present era of intense exploration of new instrumental techniques, specific pitches on the membranophones were limited to timpani and to especially tuned tom-toms and bongos. More recently, however, experimental composers have been intrigued with the possibility of altering the tone of a nonpitched drum while striking it. This is accomplished by exerting pressure on the skin with the hand, fingers, or elbow, depending upon the size of the drumhead. The pressure increases the tension of the stretched membrane or plastic surface and thus raises the normal pitch of the drum. A rising scale of pitches can be obtained by a slow and progressively heavier pressure exerted on the drumhead; a descending scale can be achieved by beginning with heavy pressure and then gradually relaxing it.

Recent scores that require this new percussion technique include:

G. Crumb: *Echoes of Time and the River*
H. Farberman: *Alea*
S. Hodkinson: *Fresco*
K. Penderecki: *Fluorescences*
R. Reynolds: *Quick are the Mouths of Earth*
G. Rochberg: *Tableaux*

G. Schuller: *Contours; Spectra*
W. Szalonek: *Concertino per flauto*

Relative pitches in ascending or descending order can also be obtained from an array of membrane and wood instruments, graded in size and position. Thus, a rising "scale" might be suggested by striking in turn the following sequence of instruments: bass drums (large, small), tom-toms (low, medium, high), tenor drum, temple-blocks (set of 5, from low to high), snare drum with snares off, woodblocks (low, medium, high), claves, and—finally—slapstick. Striking these instruments in reverse order would, of course, simulate a series of descending pitches.

Until recent years it did not seemingly occur to orchestrators that the bass drum might be "tuned" by tightening or slackening the drumhead, usually before rather than during actual playing on the instrument; see, for example, *Siebengesang* of Heinz Holliger and *Tenebrae* of Klaus Huber. Presumably, the two heads of the bass drum could be tuned differently and struck simultaneously with two beaters. The latter specification does occur, of course, in several twentieth-century scores (including Harrison Birtwistle's *Nomos* and my own *Los Dioses Aztecas*), but without specifying different tunings.

Just as a series of relative pitches can be suggested by the tones elicited from various-sized drums, so high, medium, and low pitches may be suggested by a seried group of hung cymbals, gongs, and other metallic instruments, scaled from large to small. A descending order of pitches, for instance, could be approximated by striking the following sequence of metal instruments: small triangle, crotale, large triangle, suspended cymbals (3 or more, arranged from high to low), high gong, deep tam-tam. Other analogous groups can easily be formulated, utilizing only the unpitched percussion, to suggest gradated scales of indefinite but relative pitch.

There are still other ways by which the metallic percussion can be made to create the illusion of changing tessitura. One method is to immerse the instrument in a tub of water after striking it; aptly termed "water gongs," they are required in:

J. Cage: *First Construction (in Metal)*
J. Cage, L. Harrison: *Double Music*
G. Crumb: *Echoes of Time and the River*
F. Evangelisti: *Spazio a5*
P. Méfano: *Lignes*

These are merely ordinary Chinese gongs, suspended by a cord, which the player slowly lowers into a tub of water after, or while, striking with various stipulated beaters. When the vibrating gong is immersed, the pitch is depressed slightly; when the gong is lifted out of the water, the pitch appears to rise somewhat.

A pitch change can also be simulated by applying a metal object (a thin rod, a coin, a wirebrush, and the like) to the vibrating rim of suspended cymbal, gong, or tam-tam—an effect requisitioned in:

G. Crumb: *Echoes of Time and the River*
L. Foss: *Elytres*
K. Penderecki: *Dimensions of Time and Silence*
G. Read: *Haiku Seasons*

New Areas of Striking

Twentieth-century scores are customarily very precise about indicating the area on which a percussionist should strike a membrane or metallic instrument. On occasion one finds directions to hit the frame, shell, or casing of these various instruments instead of the normal surface. On timpani, for instance, the player may be required to strike the kettle (or bowl) with regular timpani mallets or other objects, or to hit the metal rim surrounding the drumhead. On old-fashioned, hand-tuned drums he could also strike the tuning screws. The following works contain one or the other of these requirements:

M. Colgrass: *As Quiet As*
D. Erb: *Concerto for Solo Percussionist; Symphony of Overtures,* and other works
F. Evangelisti: *Ordini*
R. L. Finney: *Three Studies in Fours*
M. Geilen: *Musica*
S. Hodkinson: *Fresco*
M. Kagel: *Sonant*
W. Kotonski: *Musica per fiati e timpani*
L. Kupkovic: *Das Fleisch des kreuzes*
G. Ligeti: *Apparitions*
G. Read: *Los Dioses Aztecas*
D. Reck: *Blues and Screamer*
H. Villa-Lobos: *Danses Africaines*
B. A. Zimmermann: *Canto di speranza*

The metal rims and the wood or metal casings of the smaller drums—snare, tenor, bongos, tom-toms, and so on—as well as of the larger bass drum, can all be struck in some manner. The sounds will vary according to the size of the drum, the part of the casing hit, and the agent used. An impressive variety of objects have been designated by vanguard orchestrators for striking the outsides of the various drums: the wood end of a regular mallet, metal rods, wire-brushes, crotale, cymbal, clave, maraca, and other equally exotic agents of attack. These specifications may be observed in the following scores:

S. Bussotti: *Memoria*
D. Erb: *The Seventh Trumpet; Symphony of Overtures*
L. Ferrari: *Société II*
G. Heussenstamm: *Poikilos*
M. Kagel: *Anagrama; Sonant*
J. Moross: *Paeans*
K. Penderecki: *Dimensions of Time and Silence; Fluorescences,* and other works
G. Read: *Los Dioses Aztecas*
S. Revueltas: *Sensemayá*
K. Serocki: *Continuum; Episodes*
E. Varèse: *Intégrales*

On occasion the metal frame or the resonators under the plates of vibraphone, marimba, or xylophone have been designated for percussive attack (non-glissando), either with regular mallets or the wood end of a stick (see *Scultura* of Boguslaw Schäffer, for example).

Unusual Agents of Attack

Directions to percussionists for employing different kinds of mallets and beaters are as common in contemporary scores as the designations of surface area to be struck; hence they need no further explication here. Even the mallet symbology has achieved a measure of concurrence:

$\mathbf{\uparrow}$ = hard sticks, $\mathbf{\uparrow}$ = soft sticks, $\mathbf{\ddagger}$ = wire brushes

Vanguard orchestrators are notably partial to the use of the player's fingertips and nails in creating delicate sounds on membranophones and idiophones alike. Somewhat more robust sounds are achieved, of course, by the use of the flat hands or the knuckles on the drum surfaces. The following are some of the stipulations to be found in recent compositions:

1. Tap, roll, or strike on the drum surface with the fingertips

   T. Baird: *Etiuda*

   R. S. Brindle: *Auriga*

   S. Bussotti: *Mit einem gewissen sprechenden Ausdruck*

   M. Colgrass: *As Quiet As; Six Allegro Duets*

   G. Crumb: *Echoes of Time and the River*

   H. Farberman: *Alea*

   L. Foss: *Fragments of Archilochos*

   O. Henry: *Do Not Pass Go*

   G. Heussenstamm: *Seventeen Impressions*

   M. Kagel: *Sonant*

   W. Kotonski: *Musica per fiati e timpani*

   D. Martino: *Piano Concerto*

   L. de Pablo: *Reciprico*

   G. Read: *Los Dioses Aztecas*

   M. Stibilj: *Condensation*

   W. Sydeman: *Study for Orchestra No. III; Trio for Flute, Double Bass and Percussion*

2. Same, with the flat hand

   D. Burge: *Sources III*

   S. Bussotti: *Mit einem gewissen sprechenden Ausdruck*

   E. Carter: *Eight Pieces for Four Timpani*

   R. L. Finney: *Concerto for Percussion; Three Studies in Fours*

   O. Henry: *Do Not Pass Go*

   W. Kotonski: *Musica per fiati e timpani*

   M. Mestres-Quadreny: *Tramesa a Tapies*

   W. Sydeman: *Trio for Flute, Double Bass and Percussion*

3. Same, with the knuckles

   L. de Pablo: *Reciprico*

4. Scratch or strike on the drumhead with the fingernails

   B. Childs: *Music for Bass Drum*

   M. Colgrass: *As Quiet As*

   P. M. Davies: *Eight Songs for a Mad King*

   D. Erb: *Symphony of Overtures*

   M. Kagel: *Anagrama; Sonant*

   K. Penderecki: *Dimensions of Time and Silence*

   G. Read: *Los Dioses Aztecas*

   R. Reynolds: *Quick are the Mouths of Earth*

R. M. Schafer: *Requiems for the Party-Girl*
M. Stibilj: *Condensation*

5. "Write" on the drumhead with the fingernail

   M. Kagel: *Anagrama; Sonant*

6. Rub on the drumhead with the fingers

   J. Druckman: *Animus 2*
   C. Halffter: *Fibonaciana*
   G. Read: *Los Dioses Aztecas*

7. Same, with the flat hand or the fist

   H. Farberman: *Alea*
   M. Kagel: *Sonant*
   K. Penderecki: *Fluorescences*
   M. Stibilj: *Condensation*

8. Roll, strike, or tap on the bars of the idiophones (vibraphone, marimba, etc.) with the fingertips

   M. Finnissy: *As When Upon a Tranced Summer Night*
   G. Read: *Haiku Seasons*
   W. Sydeman: *Trio for Flute, Double Bass and Percussion*

9. Same, with the fingernails

   G. Crumb: *Madrigals—I*
   G. Read: *Haiku Seasons*

10. Same, with the palm or flat hand

    G. Amy: *Cycle*

11. Roll, strike, or tap on suspended cymbal, gong, or tam-tam with the fingertips

    G. Crumb: *Echoes of Time and the River*
    L. Foss: *Fragments of Archilochos*
    L. de Pablo: *Reciprico*
    G. Read: *Haiku Seasons*

12. Same, with the flat hand

    G. Arrigo: *Thumos*
    J. Druckman: *Animus 2*
    R. L. Finney: *Three Studies in Fours*
    V. Globokar: *Accord*
    M. Kagel: *Anagrama*

D. Martino: *Piano Concerto*

M. Mestres-Quadreny: *Tramesa a Tapies*

G. Read: *Haiku Seasons; Los Dioses Aztecas*

13. Same, with the fingernails

M. Finnissy: *As When Upon a Tranced Summer Night*

L. Foss: *Time Cycle*

M. Kagel: *Anagrama*

14. Tap on a maraca with the fingers

D. Banks: *Tirade*

In his unusual *Music for Bass Drum*, Barney Childs gives elaborate instructions for snapping or flicking the nails on the flat part of the drum tuning handle, the edge of the shell, near to the tie rod, and at the membrane node. Further specifications are to tap with the ball of the finger at the drumhead edge and on the flat part of the wooden rim; also, to roll with the fingers on both shell and skin; tap with the nails at the middle of the casing and on the drumhead, and rap with the knuckles on skin, tuning handle, and tie rod.

Highly intriguing in sonic terms are the special sounds available to the orchestrator when timpani and other drums are struck not with standardized sticks and mallets but with such exotic objects as a clave, maraca, woodblock, triangle, tambourine, or hand cymbal, as well as with sleigh-bells and chains. In actuality, these striking procedures convey a two-fold aural impression to the listener—the percussive impact of the unusual agent on the instrument membrane and the inherent sound of the object itself.

A few of the bizarre effects demanded by experimental composers include the following:

1. Play close to the timpani rims with thin triangle beaters

H. Brant: *Verticals Ascending*

2. Play on drum surface with chains (dragged across the drumhead, or dropped onto it)

H. W. Henze: *Sinfonia N. 6*

3. Same, with a plastic fly swatter

B. Childs: *Nonet*

4. "Write" name and address with tip of snare drum stick on the drumhead

B. Childs: *Jack's New Bag*

5. Press the thick end of a snare drum stick down on the drumhead and drag it across from rim to rim

    G. Read: *Los Dioses Aztecas* (Example 31)

6. Rub or scrape in a rotary motion on the drumhead with a wirebrush

    H. Badings: *Symphonische Klangfiguren*
    D. Bedford: *Piece for Mo*
    J. Cage: *Amores*
    S. Cervetti: *Six Sequences*
    W. Duckworth: *Gambit*
    J. C. Eloy: *Equivalences*
    E. Raxach: *Estrofas*
    G. Read: *Los Dioses Aztecas*

7. Scrape a dull knife blade across the drumhead

    R. Reynolds: *Quick are the Mouths of Earth*

8. Rub the surface of the drum with a hairbrush

    A. Mellnäs: *Aura*

9. Same, with sandpaper blocks

    G. Read: *Los Dioses Aztecas*

10. Same, with a piece of aluminum paper while crushing it

    C. Alsina: *Trio 1967*

11. Stroke the surface of snare drum (snares off) with two cloths

    G. Ligeti: *Aventures*

12. Ru a rosined glove or cloth over a snare drum stick whose tip is pressed against the center of a bass drumhead

    W. Russell: *Fugue for Eight Percussion Instruments*

13. Strike the underneath rim of a cymbal laid curved side down on a timpano head

    W. Kotonski: *a battere* (Example 32)

14. Lay a string of sleighbells on the flat bass drum; play normally on the drumhead

    N. T. Dao: *Máy*

15. Lay the bottom bar of a triangle on the timpano head; strike the triangle while moving the drum pedal up and down

    D. Erb: *The Seventh Trumpet*

Example 31 Gardner Read: from *Los Dioses Aztecas* (p. 9)

Example 32 Wlodsimierz Kotonski: from *a battere* (p. 17)

172

16. Spin a silver dollar on the timpano head, making a slow glissando with the pedal at the same time

    M. Ellis: *Mutations*

17. Spin a coin (silver dollar, quarter, etc.) on the drumhead (snare, tenor, tom-tom, etc.)

    B. Childs: *Jack's New Bag*
    V. Globokar: *Accord*
    M. Kagel: *Sonant*
    M. Mestres-Quadreny: *Tramesa a Tapies*

18. Get any wind-up mechanical toy which hops or jumps; wind it up and let it hop about on a timpano surface

    B. Childs: *Jack's New Bag*

Dropping an object onto the surface of timpani or the other drums, as well as on the bars of the idiophones, is a device much favored today. The objects used range from coins of various sizes, small hand cymbals or crotales, steel balls or marbles, chains, cowbells, tambourine, rubber erasers, to sticks and rods of different materials and sizes. These requirements appear in:

C. Alsina: *Trio 1967*
L. Ferrari: *Société II*
L. Foss: *Echoi*
V. Globokar: *Accord*
M. Kagel: *Sonant*
B. Schäffer: *Scultura*

In Merrill Ellis's *Mutations* the timpanist is instructed to drop a tennis ball on the drumhead from a height of two feet, letting it bounce freely on the surface (and on to the floor?).

An even more drastic effect—visually and acoustically—is obtained by dropping instruments such as cymbal, cowbell, or tambourine on the floor or onto a tabletop (as in Alsina's *Trio* and Stravinsky's *Petrouchka*).

Recent and unorthodox methods of playing on the metal plates and wooden bars of the idiophones include striking them with a hand cymbal, finger crotale, coin, or other metal object:

E. Brown: *Available Forms 1*
L. Foss: *Echoi; Elytres*

M. Kagel: *Anagrama; Match*
B. Schäffer: *Scultura*

An increasing number of composers of experimental music have directed
the idiophone players to draw a well-rosined cello or doublebass bow across the
near edge of a metal plate on vibraphone and glockenspiel or a wooden bar of
xylophone or marimba. On the vibraphone this action produces a disembodied,
singing tone; on the marimba it creates a breathy, almost husky sound. Standing in his normal position in front of the instrument, the player can bow only on
the "white-note" (or front) plates; to bow the rear, "black-note" bars he must
stand behind the instrument. It is quite possible, of course, to utilize two
players, one for the natural pitches and one for the chromatic notes. Composers
who have made use of this very effective technique include:

I. Anhalt: *Foci*
L. Austin: *The Maze*
S. Garant: *Phrases I*
C. Halffter: *Fibonaciana; Planto por las victimas de la violencia* (Example 33)
W. Russell: *Fugue for Eight Percussion Instruments*
A. Woodbury: *Remembrances*

Also greatly favored by vanguardists is the sound of vibraphone or glockenspiel played with knitting needles—a delicate and highly refined percussive
effect: see:

L. Austin: *The Maze*
G. Read: *Haiku Seasons*

The tubular chimes have also come in for their share of unorthodox performance techniques: for example, they have been struck on the upper edges of the
tubes with a pair of claves (in *Anagrama* of Kagel), and clashed together with
the player's hands or outstretched arms (required in Kagel's score and in *The
Jerusalem Chagall Windows* of Jacob Gilboa). Several composers have called
for the player to blow into the tube opening, creating a delicate "whoosh"; see
Alsina's *Trio* and the *Chamber Piece* of Zbigniew Bujarski.

Highly welcome newcomers to the percussion section are the various wind
chimes, made of bamboo, metal, or glass. Ordinarily, they are set in motion by a
sweep of the flat fingers or a stick, but in *Voie* of Vinko Globokar and *Máy* of
Nguyen Thien Dao the composers request the percussionist to agitate the
chimes with both hands. Reginald Smith Brindle in *Orion M. 42* and Bruno

Example 33   Cristobal Halffter: from *Planto por las victimas de la violencia* (p. 30)

Maderna in his first oboe concerto ask the player to grasp the chimes with one hand. In *The Edge of the Land* Charles Boone directs that the chimes be "smashed together" by holding them tightly with the two hands so that they do not continue to vibrate. Roger Reynolds asks that the wind chimes be blown upon in *Wedge*—a logical directive!—and that they be stroked with a ruler in *Quick are the Mouths of Earth.*

Many contemporary composers specify that drums or hanging cymbals, gongs, or tam-tams, be struck alternately or simultaneously with two different kinds of sticks, either in each hand.[1] At other times two similar instruments are to be struck, again alternately or concurrently, with two contrasting mallet types; for example, high suspended cymbal hit with a snare drum stick and low cymbal with wirebrush. These instrumentational devices appear in:

[1] An early prototype of this action appears in the finale of Mahler's seventh symphony (1908): the bass drum is struck simultaneously with a birch switch and a sponge-headed mallet.

I. Dan: *The Silk Road*
H. Farberman: *Alea*
G. Read: *Los Dioses Aztecas*
R. Reynolds: *Wedge*
K. Stockhausen: *Kreuzspiel*
B. A. Zimmermann: *Photoptosis*

A certain amount of mallet and stick "borrowing" is quite common in today's scores. That is to say, some percussion instruments are played upon with beaters ordinarily employed on other instruments. The chimes, for instance, might be struck with vibraphone mallets, or the marimba bars struck with hard felt timpani sticks. The glockenspiel or vibraphone might be played upon with a triangle beater or with snare drum sticks, to cite only a few of the many possibilities existing for such mallet exchanges.

New Methods of Striking

An effect common to both the pitched mallet instruments and the membranophones is known as the "dead stick" technique: the mallet is not allowed to rebound from the plate or drum surface after striking, but is kept pressed down. The result is a curiously dead and muffled sound, somewhat akin to *sons étouffées* on harp or finger-muted tones on piano strings. The technique is prominently used in the following works:

P. Boulez: *Éclat*
E. Brown: *Available Forms 1; Hodograph 1*
E. Carter: *Eight Pieces for Four Timpani*
G. Crumb: *Madrigals—I*
H. El-Dabh: *Mosaic No. 1*
L. Foss: *Echoi; Time Cycle*
M. Kagel: *Anagrama; Match,* and other works
W. Kraft: *Configurations*
B. Schäffer: *Music for Mi*

Certain of the percussion instruments can be struck in unorthodox positions; that is, the instrument itself can be placed unconventionally, as by turning the snare drum upside down, the snares on top (required in Kagel's *Anagrama*). With the drum in this position the player can also pluck the taut snares, *a la guitarra,* with the fingers or the nails. The tambourine may be placed on a pad and struck with sticks, with either the rim side or the flat head uppermost, a requirement appearing in my *Haiku Seasons* and *Los Dioses Aztecas.*

While rim-shots have long been staples of contemporary percussion devices, several new allied techniques have been introduced by vanguard instrumentators. One is to strike the rim and drumhead with a single stick; to accomplish this the player holds the stick at its center and strikes with a downward motion. The following works call for this specific playing technique:

L. Berio: *Sinfonia*

S. Bussotti: *Mit einem gewissen sprechenden Ausdruck*

K. Penderecki: *Anaklasis; Fluorescences,* and other works

K. Stockhausen: *Momente*

E. Varèse: *Déserts; Ecuatorial*

A variant of this technique is to lay one drumstick on the membrane and strike it with another stick; see, for example:

M. Kagel: *Sonant*

K. Penderecki: *Anaklasis; Fluorescences,* and other works

W. Russell: *Fugue for Eight Percussion Instruments*

Obviously, both of these effects are useful only at a high dynamic level. A related technique, one possible at all levels of amplitude, is to strike one snare drum stick against another, like a pair of claves; this stipulation appears in my *Los Dioses Aztecas.*

Directives for striking suspended cymbals, gongs, and tam-tams are amazingly diverse and imaginative in late twentieth-century scores. They—and all the other performance techniques catalogued here—are reliable indices of how far percussive concepts have developed since the pioneering explorations of Bartók, Milhaud, and Varèse, not to mention the most recent probings of Cage, Crumb, Kagel, and Penderecki. It would be quite literally impossible to enumerate all of the unusual directions to be found in recent scores relating to playing on the metallic percussion; those that are listed below are representative samplings, and will surely provide the orchestrator with substantial food for thought.

Striking procedures on these instruments can be unconventional in the area to be struck, the agent used for playing, or both. In the first category would fit the following instructions culled from recently published compositions:

1. Play on both surfaces of gong or tam-tam simultaneously
   F. Cerha: *Relazioni fragili*
   H. Farberman: *Alea*

Rarely used, but quite possible, is the device of striking the centers of both sides of gong or tam-tam with the clenched fist of one hand and a regular beater in the other.

2. Strike edge of suspended cymbal with a stick held at right angles to the rim
   D. Bedford: *Piece for Mo*

3. Scrape the bottom surface of suspended cymbal with a metal (triangle) stick
   R. Moeves: *Et Occidentum Illustra*

4. Rub the rim of suspended cymbal with a metal stick
   M. Ishi: *Sieben Stücke*
   L. de Pablo: *Reciprico*

5. Rub the two cymbals together in a circular, irregular movement
   P. Méfano: *Paraboles*

6. Rub the bottom bar of a triangle with the metal beater
   K. Serocki: *Niobe*

Under the second category—unorthodox agents of percussive attack on the metallic instruments—one might list:

1. Draw the edge of a fingernail across the surface of suspended cymbal
   K. Penderecki: *Dimensions of Time and Silence*

2. Same, with hand and a finger ring simultaneously
   C. Alsina: *Trio 1967*

3. Roll or trill on suspended cymbal, triangle, cowbell, gong, or tam-tam with knitting needles
   L. Austin: *The Maze*
   W. Fortner: *Mouvements*
   H. W. Henze: *4. Sinfonie*
   G. Read: *Haiku Seasons*
   E. Toch: *3rd Symphony*
   I. Yun: *Dimensionen*

4. Scrape surface of suspended cymbal with a coin

   G. Crumb: *Ancient Voices of Children; Madrigals—IV*

5. Dangle chains on surface of iron (suspended) cymbal

   H. W. Henze: *Sinfonia N. 6*

6. Strike suspended cymbal with a triangle

   W. Walton: *Façade*

7. Strike suspended cymbal with back edge of a saw blade; also draw a saw blade, teeth down, across the surface or rim of suspended cymbal

   W. Russell: *Three Dance Movements*

8. Rub or stroke surface of suspended cymbal with the tips of a hard rubber comb

   R. Reynolds: *Blind Men*

9. Rub surface of gong with head of vibraphone mallet

   L. Foss: *Echoi*

10. Strike gong with a hand cymbal

    W. Haupt: *Volume*
    M. Kagel: *Anagrama*

11. Same, with a maraca

    L. de Pablo: *Reciprico*

12. Press a woodblock against tam-tam ; strike other surface with a clave

    M. Kagel: *Anagrama*

13. Rub tam-tam with a cardboard tube to make a whistling sound

    D. Burge: *Sources III*

14. Scrape surface of tam-tam with the four open edges of one half of a metal tea container (canister) of medium size

    I. Anhalt: *Foci*

15. Rub back of tam-tam (like a tambourine thumb-roll) with rubber finger-tip; also flick surface with a fingernail

    R. O'Donnell: *Microtimbre I*

16. Stroke a glass vase (or a piece of glass) over the surface of the tam-tam

    J-Y. Bosseur: *Un arraché de partout*
    C. Halffter: *Fibonaciana*

17. Scrape the teeth of a guiro (rasper) over the rim of the tam-tam with one hand while striking the center with a stick in the other hand

    F. Miroglio: *Réfractions*

18. Strike triangle with a tenpenny nail

    G. Crumb: *Ancient Voices of Children*

19. Trill on triangle with a wirebrush

    W. Sydeman: *Trio for Flute, Double Bass and Percussion*

20. Same, with a ¹⁄₁₆″ airplane wire, long enough to be "whippy"

    B. Childs: *Jack's New Bag*

Performance directives that involve both an unusual instrument area to be struck on the metal instruments and a novel agent to be utilized include the following:

1. Using the thick end of a snare drum stick, drag it slowly around the circumference of the suspended cymbal

   G. Read: *Los Dioses Aztecas* (Example 31)

2. Agitate a suspended cymbal with its rim between the wires of a wirebrush

   Z. Bujarski: *Kinoth*

3. Enclose (by clapping together) the rim of suspended cymbal with a slapstick

   M. Kagel: *Anagrama*

4. Slide in a continual circle at the center of gong or tam-tam with a triangle beater

   D. Burge: *Sources III*
   J. Druckman: *Dark Upon the Harp; Incenters,* and other works
   H. W. Henze: *Sinfonia N. 6*
   A. Nordheim: *Response I*
   E. Raxach: *Paraphrase*
   G. Read: *Los Dioses Aztecas*
   I. Stravinsky: *Le Sacre du Printemps*

5. Strike rim of tam-tam with snare drum sticks

   G. Crumb: *Echoes of Time and the River*

6. Slowly slide (or rub) triangle beater around outer edge of suspended cymbal, gong, or tam-tam

    M. Ishi: *Aphorismen*

    L. de Pablo: *Reciprico*

    E. Raxach: *Estrofas*

    G. Read: *Haiku Seasons*

7. Tremolo on a cymbal plate [suspended] with a cello bow

    A. Schoenberg: *Five Pieces for Orchestra*

8. Stroke (with a vertical upwards motion) the rim of gong, tam-tam, cowbell, or hand-held cymbal with a cello or doublebass bow

    W. Albright: *Danse Macabre*

    C. Alsina: *Symptom*

    P. Chihara: *Willow, Willow*

    B. Childs: *Jack's New Bag*

    R. Gerhard: *Concerto for Orchestra*

    C. Halffter: *Noche Pasiva del Sentido; Planto por las victimas de la violencia* (Example 33)

    S. Hodkinson: *Fresco*

    R. O'Donnell: *Microtimbre I*

    K. Penderecki: *Dimensions of Time and Silence*

    R. Reynolds: *Blind Men; Quick are the Mouths of Earth*

    G. Rochberg: *Tableaux*

    A. Woodbury: *Remembrances*

    B. A. Zimmermann: *Photoptosis*

By changing the degree of bowing pressure and the speed at which the bow is moved across the rim, a simulation of pitch change can be produced.

9. Rub the edges (upper rims) of the chime bars with a metal stick

    G. Self: *Warwick*

The British composer Richard Meale, in his *Clouds now and then*, directs that after the gong has been struck, the percussionist must sway to and fro the metal bar from which the gong is hung. This action is analogous to the shaking of a pair of cymbals after having clashed them together (see page 33) in that a faint but discernible oscillation of pitch can be perceived.

A final category comprises not only unusual areas and agents of percussion attack but highly unconventional "instruments" as well; a prime example is the directive in Peter Maxwell Davies' *Revelation and Fall* to rub the edge of a knife blade over a wet sheet of glass.

Tremoli Variants

In many recent scores several new tremolando effects have been applied to the pitched mallet instruments. One such device is a tremolo between two of the suspended tubes (resonators) of vibraphone or marimba, usually with a metal rod or the wood end of a mallet (see Kazimierz Serocki's *Continuum*, and *Fantasmagoria*, for example). In *Epifanie* Luciano Berio asks for a simultaneous tremolo on both the upper and lower surfaces of a marimbaphone bar—on the "white-note" row for player 1 and on the "black-note" row for player 2, who is stationed on the far side of the instrument. The actual procedure is best explained in the composer's own words: "The player should hold two very soft sticks in each hand . . . like a fork—one stick over and one under the end of the keys. The notes are to be quickly tremoloed in such a way that . . . the sticks strike alternately against the upper and lower side of the keys." There is no reason, of course, why this technique could not easily be transferred to the other idiophones.

A technique strictly limited to the vibraphone is turning the motor or fan on or off at the very moment of striking the plates, or after the plate has been struck and the tone is still sounding; see:

D. Burge: *Sources III*
G. Read: *Haiku Seasons*

Also confined to the peculiar mechanism of the vibraphone is fastening down the pedal so that any or all of the struck tones vibrate to maximum duration, while leaving the performer free to move about without hindrance (as in Sydney Hodkinson's *Fresco*).

Idiophone Clusters

It should be evident that the idiophones alone among all the percussion instruments have the capacity of producing cluster sounds. Formerly, these closely knit sonorities—indeed, all so-called "chords"—were restricted on the mallet instruments to not more than six notes, three to either hand. Only under optimum conditions (ample time for positioning the mallets in either hand and chords that were conveniently spaced) was the player able to strike more than three pitches in either hand. But with the recent invention of "cluster-sticks" (mallets shaped like a T, the stem being their handles and the top crossbar their striking areas, the latter varying between 17 and 25 cm in width), the player is able to hit from two to five plates with either hand if the pitches are in diatonic order. On glockenspiel, more than five bars can be struck simultaneously with either hand, owing to the smaller width of the metal plates. Among the new scores requiring the use of cluster-sticks are:

D. Bedford: *Piece for Mo*
R. Reynolds: *Quick are the Mouths of Earth*
K. Serocki: *Continuum; Fantasmagoria,* and other works

Yet other methods have been devised to produce idiophone clusters: in *Apparitions,* for instance, Ligeti asks the player to strike as many plates as possible with two rulers held horizontally. In Kagel's *Anagrama,* glockenspiel clusters are to be played with a metal rod, also held horizontally, and later with a cymbal clashed on the plates. The composer likewise instructs a percussionist to strike as many contiguous chime tubes as possible with a pair of hand cymbals, moved in a circular motion.

Finally, in George Crumb's *Madrigals—Book I,* the vibraphonist is directed to strike the instrument damper bar so sharply that all the plates vibrate sympathetically, creating a three-octave chromatic-cluster simulation.

Miscellaneous Effects

The American and European orchestrator has by now greatly enlarged his percussive resources by frequently bringing into the section instruments indigenous to other parts of the world. From Latin America he has appropriated bongos, cabacas, chocolo, conga drums, claves, cuica, guiro, maracas, reco-reco, and timbales; from Africa he has borrowed darabukas, log and slit drums, and thumb piano; from the Far East he has imported bamboos, elephant bells, Indian hand bells, koto, sho, tablas, Thailand gongs, and Tibetan prayer stones. Not content with these exotica, however, he has also requisitioned such rarities as the following:

1. Elastic bands of various thicknesses and tension to snap; a large, thick book whose pages are to be riffled; a tightly filled cushion to be struck with a carpet-beater;

a resonant piece of furniture to be struck with a cudgel; a paper bag to be inflated and exploded; a suitcase with a rough surface to be stroked with emery paper

G. Ligeti: *Aventures*

2. Sheets of paper to be torn apart; a thick carpet, suspended, to be struck with a straw rug-beater; a tin can to be smashed with a hammer; a wooden lath to be broken in two; a plastic cup to be crushed; an inflated balloon to be stroked with wet fingers; a toy tin frog which makes a loud creaking to activate; a large bottle to be smashed against an iron plate; a silk cloth to be torn apart; a metal tray filled with dishes to smash; a wooden bowl filled with marbles to rattle; paper-thin metal foils to be softly fluttered

G. Ligeti: *Nouvelles Aventures*

3. An inflated balloon to be rubbed and popped in palms of hands; an automobile horn (battery operated or on tape) to sound; two iron pipes to be struck with a third pipe; a framed piece of glass to be scratched on with the rim of a hard plastic container; a pistol with blanks or a cap pistol to fire off; a bottle to be blown on (tuned to A220); a bulbous type bicycle horn to be honked; a police-, dog-, and slide-whistle to blow; a duck horn to sound; a transistor radio to play; a large piece of glass to be broken

A. Curran: *Home-made*

4. A saw to rub with a cello bow; a metal coil to twang; a washboard to rub; a garbage can cover to strike; a tree stump to hit with an axe; several salad bowls to strike; a large crate to smash; a bag of steel pipes to pour into a steel barrel; several door bells to ring; a player piano to pump; some toy noisemakers to sound; several music boxes to turn on

L. Austin: *The Maze*

This listing by no means exhausts the unusual percussive "instruments" to be encountered in the avant-garde scores of the last few years. The point is well made, nonetheless, that today anything and everything is grist for the orchestrational mill. As John Cage prophesied in 1937: "I believe that the use of noise to make music will continue and increase . . . any and all sounds that can be heard will be made available for musical purposes." No one can argue that his prediction has come to pass in ways that surely even Cage did not anticipate.

11

HARP AND OTHER PLUCKED INSTRUMENTS

Of the specific harp effects catalogued throughout this book, most were invented, or indirectly influenced, by the Franco-American harpist and composer Carlos Salzedo. No modern instrument, not even a member of the vastly enlarged percussion family, has undergone such a metamorphosis in the twentieth century as the harp. The transformation is not in terms of the harp's construction or basic performing technique but in the vanguard orchestrators' conception of what the instrument can and should do in the milieu of experimental music. To compare the earlier harp writing of Hector Berlioz with that of the later Impressionists—Claude Debussy in *La Mer* or *Jeux,* let us say—is to understand clearly that the one composer defined the harp's physiognomy and the other its psychology. But to compare the demands made by Debussy, Ravel, or Salzedo himself with those currently operative in the scores of Bussotti, Kagel, Berio, or Bernard Rands, for example, is to hear a new definition of harp sound—no longer the delicate embodiment of grace and tonal refinement once thought to be the ultimate characteristic of the instrument, but a modern tonal agent almost totally new in terms of timbre and technical scope.

Pedal Glissandi and Trills

Standard glissandi variants and novel percussive devices alike, as applied to the harp, have been discussed on earlier pages, as have muting techniques and microtonal tunings. Here we deal with some remaining aspects of modern harp usage, such as unconventional manipulations of the pedals. One effect currently favored is to instruct the harpist constantly to change the pedal positions in a random order, usually in the context of a continual glissando or a chord bisbigliando; see:

> L. Berio: *Chemins I; Sequenza II* (Example 4-c)
> M. Kagel: *Sonant* (Example 9-n)
> G. Read: *Haiku Seasons*
> L. Schifrin: *Continuum*
> T. Takemitsu: *Eucalypts (I)*

Another technique is for the player to hold a specified pedal between two positions (flat and natural, or natural and sharp) while, or just after, the requisite string is plucked; Salzedo called this technique "metallic sounds," and it has been used by the following composers:

> L. Berio: *Chemins II; Epifanie,* and other works
> F. Cerha: *Relazioni fragili*
> D. Erb: *Concerto for Solo Percussionist*
> B. Jolas: *Tranche*
> S. Matsushita: *Fresque sonore*
> F. Miroglio: *Réseaux*
> B. Rands: *Actions for six; Formants I*
> G. Read: *Haiku Seasons*
> E. Varèse: *Ameriques; Offrandes*

The same effect may also be accomplished by releasing a pedal from one of the notches so slowly that it stays in half-position (as in Ligeti's *Apparitions*). In addition, after plucking a string, the harpist may depress its pedal in such a way that the vibrating string strikes against the tuning pins, creating a distinct "buzz"; refer to:

> M. Kagel: *Sonant*
> W. Szalonek: *Concertino per flauto*

Pedal glissandi and trills are feasible new techniques and have been utilized by a number of contemporary orchestrators. To achieve the former effect, the string is first plucked and then the corresponding pedal is immediately and fully raised or depressed. To raise the pedal from the lowest to the highest notch creates a descending slide of a whole tone, while to depress it from highest to lowest notch produces an ascending whole-step glissando. Among many works calling for this technique may be cited:

A. Bancquart: *Palimpsestes*
D. Banks: *Tirade*
S. Barber: *Souvenirs*
S. Bussotti: *Fragmentations*
G. Crumb: *Madrigals—IV*
D. Erb: *Concerto for Solo Percussionist*
R. Felciano: *Background Music*
L. Foss: *Elytres; Orpheus*
R. Gerhard: *Concerto for Orchestra*
K. Huber: *des Engels anredung an die seele*
M. Kagel: *Anagrama; Sonant* (Example 9-j), and other works
F. Miroglio: *Réseaux*
R. Moeves: *Et Occidentum Illustra*
G. Read: *Toccata Giocosa*
J. Serebrier: *Colores Magicos*

The pedal trill is achieved by plucking a specified string and then moving the corresponding pedal up and down as quickly as possible and for as long as the sound persists; see:

L. Berio: *Sequenza II*
M. Kagel: *Sonant*
Y. Sadai: *Nuances*

The ultimate in pedal effects is undoubtedly Salzedo's "esoteric sounds": the player moves all the pedals in random order and a vigorously as possible but does not play on the strings. The aural result of this balletic activity is a subdued percussive rustle, though it is clear that both Berio (in *Sequenza II*) and Bussotti in his *Fragmentations* (Example 34) had a visual goal in mind as well.

Example 34   Sylvano Bussotti: from *Fragmentations* (p. 1)

188

Tuning-key and Tuning-pin Effects

In addition to inventing the tuning-key glissando, discussed on page 38, Salzedo also devised other ways of employing this necessary agent in performance. To achieve his "fluidic sounds" the harpist places the center of the tuning key against the very top of the string, which is plucked near to the soundboard. Another playing method, called "rocket-like sounds," follows the same procedure, but the tuning key is quickly slid along the string as it is plucked. A few of Salzedo's solo harp pieces utilize this device, as do Richard Felciano's *Background Music* and *Actions for six* of Bernard Rands. A closely related effect, of course, is to slide the tuning key on a bass wire string (the "fluidic glissando" described on page 38), but at the end of the slide the key is pulled abruptly from the string, plucking it with a metallic twang; see Salzedo's *Scintillation*, for example.

There are still other ways in which the tuning key may be utilized for special effects: in one, the player holds the key in his right hand, with the metal shank exerting pressure on the string which is to be plucked normally; the result is a deadening of the string's natural resonance. In addition, any string may be struck or rhythmically tapped with the key-end (as in Donald Erb's *Symphony of Overtures*), or any three or four contiguous strings can be struck with the broad wooden handle; this latter effect was called for by Salzedo in a number of his solo harp pieces. Furthermore, a plucked and still vibrating string can be lightly touched with the metal end of the tuning key, resulting in a metallic buzz; this device appears in the Erb work just cited and in Per Norgård's *Symphony No. 2*.

The tuning pegs of the harp figure prominently in several unusual effects: for instance, harpists have frequently been instructed to play high on the strings, quite close to the metal pins, in contradistinction to the normal position in the center of the strings or the more conventional requisition of *près de la table*. Playing in this position produces a thin, brittle sound, and has been exploited in the following recent compositions:

S. Bussotti: *Fragmentations*
H. Gorecki: *Monologhi*
M. Kagel: *Sonant* (Example 9-h,p)
P. Méfano: *Paraboles*
B. Rands: *Formants I*
E. Raxach: *Paraphrase*
G. Read: *Sonoric Fantasia No. 3*

And in Earle Brown's *Available Forms 2* and *Times Five,* the composer directs the harpist to play *above* the tuning pins, where pitch is indeterminate and string resonance is weak.

To effectuate Salzedo's "vibrant sounds," the left thumb presses down with rapid motions on the strings between the tuning pegs and the metal discs, while the right hand plays normally on the strings; see various of Salzedo's harp pieces, as well as Vinko Globokar's *Voie.*

Finally, in *Mit einem gewissen sprechenden Ausdruck* of Bussotti, the harpist is directed to draw a metal stick heavily along the row of tuning pins, creating a violent clacking.

Guitar, Mandolin, and Banjo techniques

As with all stringed instruments, whether fretted or not, there is a normal playing area on the strings of the guitar, mandolin, and banjo. For a change of timbre, however, some recent composers have instructed the players of these instruments to pluck the strings in unconventional locales, such as:

1. Near to or directly on the bridge

   D. Erb: *String Trio*
   L. Foss: *Fragments of Archilochos*
   R. Gerhard: *Concert for 8*
   C. Halffter: *Codex I*
   M. Kagel: *Sonant*
   G. Read: *Canzone di Notte*

2. Above (behind) the bridge

   D. Erb: *String Trio*
   L. Foss: *Fragments of Archilochos*
   M. Kagel: *Sonant*
   A. Mellnäs: *Tombola*

3. Beyond the nut or fingerboard

   L. Foss: *Fragments of Archilochos*
   M. Kagel: *Sonant*

In Gerhard's *Concert for 8,* the guitar is required to be held in an unorthodox position: to enable the strings to be played with a loosely strung, well-rosined cello bow, the instrument must be laid flat on the guitarist's lap.

Guitar strings are normally plucked with the fingertips, but some instrumentators have on occasion requested that they be plucked with other agents:

1. The fingernails

    G. Arrigo: *Tre Occasioni*
    S. Bussotti: *Memoria*
    L. Foss: *Fragments of Archilochos*
    R. Gerhard: *Concert for 8*
    M. Kagel: *Heterophonie*
    G. Read: *Canzone di Notte*

2. A plectrum or pick

    H. W. Henze: *Sinfonia N. 6* (Example 39)
    M. Kagel: *Sonant*

Contrariwise, mandolin and banjo strings are ordinarily played with special picks or plectrums. Substitute agents required in several recent scores include:

1. The fingertips

    G. Crumb: *Night of the Four Moons*
    D. Erb: *String Trio*

2. A metal rod

    G. Crumb: *Songs, Drones, and Refrains of Death* (also applied to guitar)

Although Crumb has never claimed to have invented the "bottle-neck" technique of playing on these plucked instruments, he is—at the least—the most avid practitioner of the device. "Bottle-neck" playing is accomplished by holding a glass rod lightly against the E-string (of mandolin or banjo) with the left hand; after plucking the string with a metal plectrum (a paper clip makes an excellent substitute), the player then slides the rod along the string, producing various portamento pitches. The sound is somewhat like the ondes Martenot or the Theremin, disembodied and softly wailing. For glimpses of the technique at work in a musical context refer to both the *Ancient Voices of Children* and *Night of the Four Moons* of Crumb.

Other effects on these plucked instruments, more specifically percussive in nature, have been dealt with on previous pages (72–73).

12

KEYBOARD INSTRUMENTS

One can confidently assert that with the single exception of the harp, no modern instrument favored by the musical avant-garde has been so radically altered in conception as the piano. The techniques presently applied to this instrument are poles removed from conventional keyboard methodology. It is not that the piano has become even more solidly entrenched as a percussive instrument, but rather that today's experimental composers have a new awareness of its tone-color potential. No longer is the piano considered to be monochromatic; neither does it function exclusively in a melodic/harmonic manner as it did up to the mid-point of the present century. Now, after intense experimentation by the vanguard, it has emerged as a hybrid instrument, combining elements of both tuned and unpitched percussion with certain tonal characteristics of harp and harpsichord. In this metamorphosis of the piano the deciding factor is the composer's concept of the interior areas, with less emphasis on the exterior keys. Indeed, the piano has become an instrument whose sound-producing mechanism is plucked rather than struck; the primary locale of playing has thus been transferred from the outside to the inside of the frame.

This conceptual transformation of the piano has not affected the other keyboard instruments. Because the harpsichord is a keyed instrument whose strings are plucked with quills rather than struck with felted hammers—not to mention its more delicate physique—the effects now feasible and common on the piano cannot, with few exceptions, be automatically transferred to the harpsichord's inner mechanism. And owing to their basic construction, neither the organ nor the celesta can be played upon in their interiors; any effects to be produced on these two instruments must perforce take place on their keys or on their frames.

Piano and Harpsichord Clusters

As we are concerned on these pages more with the basic timbral nature of recent pianistic devices than with their strict chronological development, the initial techniques to be discussed involve unorthodox ways of using the keys of the piano and harpsichord. Roughly graded from a more or less traditional to an experimental conception of the existing keyboard, the techniques catalogued clearly indicate the extent of the avant-gardists' search for new and viable instrumental sound effects.

Any compendium of modern instrumentational devices must include the tone-cluster, even though it is now so ubiquitous as to be a cliché. The name of Henry Cowell is most closely associated with this technique, although clusters had been used by Charles Ives, notably in the *"Concord" Sonata,* some years before Cowell's independent exploitation of this tonal device.

In their most limited form tone-clusters are produced by the bunched fingers or the flat hand on the keys; in their more extended versions they are played with the forearm (stipulated in Cowell's *Piano Concerto* of 1929) or with a mechanical contrivance such as a wooden board (as in the *"Concord" Sonata*). Recent variant forms of cluster playing include rolled or glissando clusters, the tones of the structure being progressively added to or subtracted from by the action of the flat hand or full arm. Far too many contemporary works have used this device to warrant listing here, but those given below may be considered representative:

J. Bahk: *Mark*
D. Burge: *A Song of Sixpence*
S. Bussotti: *Couple*
J. Cage: *Concert for Piano and Orchestra*
C. Cardew: *Three Winter Potatoes*
N. Castiglioni: *Cangianti*
H. Cowell: *Piano Concerto*
R. Gerhard: *Epithalamium*
A. Gilbert: *Sonata No. 2*

R. Haubenstock-Ramati: *Petite musique de nuit*

H. W. Henze: *Sinfonia N. 6*

M. Kagel: *Anagrama; Heterophonie*

M. Kelemen: *Dessins commentes*

A. Lanza: *Plectros I, II,* and other works

S. Lunetta: *Piano Music* (Example 35-a)

R. Reynolds: *Blind Men; Quick are the Mouths of Earth*

K. Stockhausen: *Gruppen; Klavierstück X,* and other works

In Stockhausen's piano piece, cited above, the composer states that in playing cluster glissandi the pianist might wear woolen gloves with the fingers cut away—presumably in consideration of the player's fingers rather than obtaining any sonic nuances.

Example 35   Stanley Lunetta: from *Piano Music* (p. 66)

Clusters produced by striking the keys with the clenched fist were first requisitioned by Cowell in such works as his 1914 *Advertisement* and, most notably, in the *Piano Concerto* of the 20's. More recent composers who have also required this performance procedure from their pianists, solo and ensemble, include:

G. Bacewicz: *Second Cello Concerto*
E. Brown: *Hodograph I*
N. T. Dao: *Tây Nguyên*
H. W. Henze: *Sinfonia N. 6*
M. Kagel: *Transición II*
M. Ohana: *Sorôn-Ngô*
K. Penderecki: *Strophes*
E. Schwartz: *Soliloquies*
K. Stockhausen: *Klavierstück X*
C. Surinach: *Symphonic Variations*
A. de la Vega: *Antinomies for Piano*

Organists, too, have been directed by contemporary composers for the instrument to play keyboard clusters with the bunched fist, notably in *Organum I* of Xavier Darasse.

In his piano piece called *Joc*, Xavier Benguerel calls for black and white key-clusters to be played with two pieces of wood, each about 50 cm in length. In my own *Haiku Seasons* the pianist is directed to hold down the lowest two octaves of white and black keys with two 15-inch rulers, while a percussionist plays on the corresponding strings with mallets. Similarly, in Maurice Ohana's *Sorôn-Ngô* several felt-backed rulers are required for holding down various cluster formations.

William Russell in his *Three Dance Movements* has the pianist depress the entire chromatic scale—all 88 keys—with a wooden board measuring $4' \times 4'' \times 1''$.[1] But perhaps the ultimate in keyboard cluster effects, visually at least, is the directive in both Theodore Lucas's *Aberrations No. VII* and *Action Music* of Alvin Lucier to sit emphatically on the keyboard.

---

[1]It is a moot point whether Russell was aware of Charles Ives' pioneering requisition of a $14\frac{3}{4}$-inch board for cluster playing in the *"Hawthorne"* movement of the *"Concord" Sonata*. At the time the *Three Dance Movements* was published (1936) the Ives work had not only not yet been publicly performed in the United States but was largely unknown except to a small group of musicians who had subscribed to the private printing of the sonata in 1921. It is extremely doubtful that Russell belonged to this group; hence his early use of a keyboard cluster-agent is a fortuitous coincidence.

Key attacks

Modern variants of traditional piano keyboard attack include the following actions:

1. Pluck the key ("plucked accent") instead of striking it, simulating pizzicato
   K. Korte: *Concerto Mutabile*

2. Strike key forcefully, staccato, and immediately depress it silently
   S. Bussotti: *Pour Clavier*
   M. Kagel: *Transición II*
   H. Pousseur: *Mobile; Rimes*
   K. Stockhausen: *Klavierstücke*
   B. A. Zimmermann: *Perspektiven*

3. Strike the key normally, then raise it (by releasing finger pressure) and depress it again silently before the sound is more than half-dampened
   A. Gilbert: *Sonata No. 2*
   R. Reynolds: *Mosaic*

4. Vibrate the key with the finger after striking it (without causing the hammer to hit the string again)
   M. Kagel: *Metapiece (Mimetics)*

5. Trill on two adjacent black keys with the knuckles
   R. Reynolds: *Blind Men*

6. As a key is pressed down with one hand, strike the palm simultaneously with the free hand
   M. Kagel: *Metapiece (Mimetics)*

7. Rapidly wriggle the fingers over the keys; silently jiggle the keys
   S. Lunetta: *Piano Music* (Example 35-b)
   L. Moss: *Omaggio*

8. Lightly strike key with flesh of finger (or with nail) without causing hammer to hit the string
   S. Bussotti: *Pour Clavier*
   M. Kagel: *Transición II*
   B. Rands: *Espressione IV*

9. Rub with the fingernails on the keys (without depressing them) with a constant and uniform movement, as fast as possible

   N. Castiglioni: *Consonante*

10. Drop a heavy wood stick onto the keys

    X. Benguerel: *Joc*

A number of composers have borrowed ideas from avant-garde organ techniques and have devised methods of keeping certain preselected piano keys depressed. For example, in *Three Winter Potatoes* Cornelius Cardew directs the pianist to insert a wedge in the crack between two white keys, one of which is depressed; a folded piece of paper or cardboard makes a satisfactory wedge. David Bedford, in *Music for Albion Moonlight,* asks for lead weights to be silently placed on certain keys to keep them down while the pianist's two hands are busy elsewhere. These devices, of course, are designed to take the place of the middle pedal in the upper keyboard area where the pedal does not function.

Pedal Effects

Aside from percussive effects with and on the three piano pedals (see page 82), many current piano works indicate varying foot pressures on the sustaining pedal: $\frac{1}{2}$, $\frac{1}{4}$, $\frac{3}{4}$, or other fractional manipulations. These requirements are seen frequently in the eleven *Klavierstücke* of Stockhausen, for instance, and in Boulez's third piano sonata and *Structures* for two pianos, among a long list of contemporary works. The use of a fluctuating (fluttering, oscillating) pedal is also a common stipulation, the player moving the pedal at different speeds and with constantly differing pressures, as in:

G. Amy: *Cahiers d'epigrammes*
W. Bolcomb: *Duets for Quintet*
M. Finnissy: *Song 9*
M. Kelemen: *Dessins commentes*
D. Lumsdaine: *Kelly Ground*
G. Rochberg: *Tableaux*

In George Crumb's *Five Pieces for Piano* the performer must strike the key forcefully, then immediately depress the damper pedal sharply; this results in a faintly audible echo of the pitch.

There is an intriguing instruction to the pianist in Jacob Druckman's *Windows*—to tap the strings with the dampers by means of a fast upward motion of the pedal; the sound is then prolonged by immediately depressing the pedal.

Kagel, in *Metapiece (Mimetics),* requires the pianist to release the sustaining pedal slowly enough that the sound of the dampers springing back can be heard, a subtle percussive addendum to the sound produced on the strings.

In Ligeti's theatrical *Nouvelles Aventures* the pianist must fasten down the sustaining pedal at one point with a wooden wedge. He does so because he is required to play in the interior with clothes brushes in either hand, standing at the left side of the instrument. Lacking a wedge, the pianist can naturally call on the services of an assistant to operate the pedal. Two other vanguard works also require the use of a pedal wedge: Istvan Anhalt's *Foci* utilizes it briefly, while in Elliott Schwartz's *Options I* it functions throughout the piece.

Interior Devices

Some piano interior effects have already been catalogued, in particular those that are primarily percussive in nature (see pages 74–83). Normally, of course, the piano strings are set in vibration by key and hammer action or by striking, plucking, or rubbing with extraneous agents—fingers, fingernails, mallets, and the like. In addition, a finger may lightly touch a string and then lift off with a sliding motion (as in Christian Wolff's *Duet I*), or may press down on a string and then release the pressure suddenly; both actions will cause the string to vibrate faintly.

What must surely be the most unusual method of setting the strings in vibration was devised by Ligeti in his *Apparitions:* the player strokes the strings with two cloths. In *Traces,* Roger Reynolds has the pianist produce shrill, ringing sounds by pressing down a plastic ruler lengthwise on the strings of the highest section and sliding it to the back.

Many contemporary composers effectively simulate harp and harpsichord tone-color on the piano by directing performers to pluck the strings with the fingernail. In addition to such percussive pluckings, already discussed (pages 74–75), certain instrumentators have requested a "metallic vibrato"; the fingernail (or a paper clip) is very lightly placed against a vibrating string, creating a delicate buzzing sound. George Crumb calls for this device in his *Five Pieces for Piano,* among other works. Furthermore, a string may be plucked with the player's nail, which is immediately turned over so as to cut off the sound with a brief metallic click (as in Wolff's *Duet I*).

In *Plectros I*, Alcides Lanza asks the pianist to raise a low, wound string with two fingers, let it twang audibly, then touch the still-vibrating string with a fingernail or a plectrum. A somewhat similar directive occurs in Donald Erb's *Concerto for Solo Percussionist:* the player is to pull up the lowest A-string, let it twang, and lay the metal tip of a pencil against it. On the other hand, Francis Miroglio requires his pianist in *Réfractions* to pinch together two low strings and let them clash one against the other, the damper pedal depressed.

A vibrating string, whether activated by key and hammer or by interior plucking, can also be lightly touched with some agent, such as a metal rod (triangle beater):

D. Erb: *Symphony of Overtures*
S. Lunetta: *Piano Music*
W. Szalonek: *Les Sons; Proporzioni II*

Furthermore, a group of contiguous vibrating strings can have a stick, dowel, metal bar, or other similar object laid across them; this action not only abruptly muffles the sound but adds a simultaneous percussive impact; see:

B. Childs: *Nonet*
A Hrisanide: *Volumes*
W. Szalonek: *Les Sons*

Various cluster effects can be created by vibrating, agitating, or rubbing some object on a group of piano strings—best achieved on the wound strings in section one (far left). The listing that follows demonstrates the ingenuity of some composers in their search for interesting new sounds:

1. A wirebrush and a piece of wood

    I. Anhalt: *Foci* (Example 15)

2. A cymbal, a tambourine, and a metal rod

    L. Ferrari: *Société II*

3. Two large clothes brushes

    G. Ligeti: *Nouvelles Aventures*

4. Bamboo sticks

    H-U. Englemann: *Cadenza*

In his *Music for Albion Moonlight*, David Bedford calls for interior clusters on the strings to be played with a T-shaped cluster stick, very similar to that used on the percussion idiophones (see page 183).

Other miscellaneous effects that involve actions within the piano interior include:

1. Hold a stiff piece of sandpaper against a string so that the hammer of an adjacent key hits the paper against the string

   B. Childs: *Jack's New Bag*

2. Stand several milk bottles (or glass tumblers) on the strings of one section and push them with the hand so that they wobble on the strings

   D. Bedford: *Come in here child; Piano Piece 2*

3. Sing, yell, speak, etc., into the piano interior with the sustaining pedal held down so that the voice is resonated by the sympathetic vibration of all the strings

   B. Childs: *Jack's New Bag*
   L. Ferrari: *Société II*
   E. Schwartz: *Music for Napoleon and Beethoven* (Example 21)

Organ Clusters and Keyboard Effects

Owing to its special construction with multiple keyboards, the organ lends itself most effectively to what might be called "transferred" clusters: the player's hand extends up from the lowest to the next higher manual, transferring the cluster formation from one to the other; or else his full arm presses down progressively on all the available manuals, in a perpendicular manner, to build up a complex sonority manual by manual. The timbres of clusters rolled in this fashion may alter progressively by means of varying registrations on the different keyboards. The organ works of Albright, Darasse, Kagel, and Ligeti, in particular, offer prime examples of this new technique.

Rolled, or glissando, clusters can be achieved on a single manual even more efficiently than on piano, celesta, or harpsichord; this is because even the slightest pressure on the organ keys makes them speak, whereas on the other instruments a weak finger pressure results in some key mechanisms not sounding the pitches.

Ordinarily, rolled and glissando clusters would be accomplished by using the flat hand, but in William Bolcom's virtuoso *Black Host* they are to be played with the clenched fist sliding across the keys.

Among a number of recent works, some for organ alone and some for the instrument used in ensemble, requiring the specialized technique of rolled and glissando clusters, one might list:

W. Albright: *Organbook II; Pneuma,* and other works
G. Cacioppo: *Holy Ghost Vacuum*
J. Druckman: *Windows*
L. Foss: *Baroque Variations*
H. W. Henze: *Sinfonia N. 6*
K. Huber: *Tenebrae*
W. Jacob: *Da Pacem*
M. Kagel: *Improvisation ajoutée*
G. Ligeti: *Volumina* (Example 36)

Also dependent upon the unique physical properties of the pipe or electronic organ are sustained clusters of long duration. Massed tones of diatonic or chromatic construction can be held ad infinitum by the player's hands or arms pressed down on the keys. To enable the organist to utilize clusters but at the same time to free his two hands for other matter, a "cluster rake" has been recently invented. This mechanical device is a 9″ board which is placed over the keys; felt-tipped knobs, spaced off on its under surface, hold down the selected keys required in the cluster. Its use makes it possible to sustain a cluster on one manual while occupying both hands on a different keyboard. Though not specified by Mauricio Kagel in his *Improvisation ajoutée,* the cluster rake is a necessity on several of its pages.

Contemporary organists also have at their disposal a newly designed cluster weight-board, a somewhat different version of the cluster rake. This device is a heavy wooden board that fits over the entire keyboard with a perforation in it over every key, black and white; lead weights are inserted in the perforations to hold down certain keys, whether contiguous or not; see:

M. Kagel: *Improvisation ajoutée*
A. Mellnäs: *Fixations*
J. W. Morthenson: *Eternes; Pour Madame Bovary*

Lacking either a cluster rake or weight-board, organists can hold down certain preselected keys by inserting thin pencil tips between the keys; obviously, sufficient time must be allowed the player to accomplish this action (as in Niccolo Castiglioni's *Sinfonie guerriere e amorose*), or else the preparation may be done by an assistant (see William Albright's *Organbook II,* for example).

A unique manner of playing cluster tremoli, on a single manual or between

Example 36 Gyorgy Ligeti: from *Volumina* (p. 10)

(13)

Right
hand

-- -- (sempre cresc.) -- cresc. molto -- -- -- *fff* -- -- great

Full organ;
all manuals
coupled to
great

R. H. and L. H. on
different manuals

No
break
in
cluster

Left
hand

-- -- (sempre cresc.) -- cresc. molto -- -- *fff*

Continue
to sustain
cluster on
great with
one Hand

Pedal

-- -- (sempre cresc.) --

202

two keyboards, is exploited in Xavier Darasse's *Organum I:* aptly and pictur-esquely called a "karaté tremolo," the action calls for the two hands to be held upright, thumbs raised, the edges of the hands literally chopping on the keyboards. Visually, the technique provides an added element of theatricality to any performance.

An unconventional keyboard effect, strictly limited to pipe organs having old-fashioned tracker action, requires the keys to be depressed partially rather than fully. This action results in the gradual emergence of sound, rather like depressing the keys of a parlor organ (harmonium) and then slowly beginning to pump the pedal. Arne Mellnäs specified this effect in his *Fixations.*

Registration Devices

Ordinarily, organ registrations are either preset or are changed during playing in carefully designated sequences or patterns. An outstanding example of patterned registration changes occurs in the *Organum I* of Darasse: one hand sustains a cluster-chord on a stipulated manual while the other alternately adds and cancels certain stops according to a very precise rhythmic sequence shown on a supplementary staff.

An increasing number of avant-garde composers of organ music are requesting random and unpatterned registrational changes, with the selection of individual stops on any one manual or on the pedal keyboard left solely to chance or to the inspiration of the moment. Consult the following works:

W. Albright: *Organbook I; Pneuma,* and other works
W. Bolcom: *Black Host*
N. Castiglioni: *Sinfonia guerriere e amorose*
R. Felciano: *Glossolalia*
A. Janson: *Canon*
M. Kagel: *Improvisation ajoutée*
G. Ligeti: *Volumina*

The organist himself is customarily responsible for changing registrations, whether planned or random, but several recent works for organ require the services of assistants to handle the changes of stops and couplers while both hands of the player are engaged on the manuals, as in:

W. Albright: *Pneuma*
X. Darasse: *Organum I*

L. Foss: *Etudes for Organ*
M. Kagel: *Improvisation ajoutée*
A. Mellnäs: *Fixations*

Restricted to the draw-stop type of console is Alfred Janson's directive in *Canon* to pull the stops out gradually; this action causes the individual stops to be activated with a little spurt of sound.

Miscellaneous Effects

Either the organist or an assistant can create a "coupler tremolo"; this is accomplished by rapidly moving one of the 16′, 8′, 4′, or 2′ manual or pedal couplers off and on while sound is being produced on the affected keyboard or on the pedals. The result is a continual adding and canceling of unison, octave, and double-octave registration from other manuals. This action is most easily handled on an instrument with coupler tabs; they have merely to be flicked up or down rather than pulled out and pushed in, as required by old-fashioned stop-knobs. *Fixations* of Arne Mellnäs is a work that makes extensive use of this technique.

Assistants are also occasionally called upon to play on manuals or pedals while the organist's two hands and feet are occupied, a performance requirement appearing in Darasse's *Organum I*.

Another novel organ technique, one that affects dynamics, is rapidly opening and closing the swell or choir shades; this action on the performer's part obviously requires that one foot is free to operate the requisite shutter pedals. As the swell and choir pedals are usually next to each other, they may be opened or closed simultaneously with one foot. Albright's *Organbook II* provides excellent examples of this idiomatic technique.

A final device, and one mechanically limited to electrically activated instruments, is the switching on or off of the motor while the manual keys and/or pedals are depressed. In the first instance the sound comes on with a sudden explosive spurt; in the second it fades away slowly as the wind is emptied from the pipes. Composers who have relied on this unique idiomatic effect include:

W. Albright: *Pneuma*
C. Cardew: *The Great Learning, Paragraph 1*
W. Jacob: *Da Pacem*
A. Janson: *Canon*
G. Ligeti: *Volumina*

A. Mellnäs: *Fixations*

J. W. Morthenson: *Eternes; Pour Madame Bovary*

K. Penderecki: *St. Luke Passion*

I. Yun: *Dimensionen*

Other than amplification, percussive blows on the instrument frame, and various tone-cluster techniques—all of which have been discussed—there is little else in the way of special effects that can be applied idiomatically to either the celesta or the harpsichord. Consequently, the score-reader will find few examples of these two instruments used in unorthodox ways.

Accordion Techniques

The free-bass accordion is a much neglected, not to say a much misunderstood and underestimated, modern instrument. In essence a miniaturized and portable reed organ, it is capable of impressive sustaining power and richness of tone and possesses a wide and flexible dynamic range. Furthermore, the free-bass accordion can produce a number of sonic effects that clearly ought to endear it to innovative composers and orchestrators. For example: in addition to chromatic manual and diminished-seventh chord button keyboard glissandi (described on page 48) and a number of unique percussive effects (see page 86), the accordion can create perceptible timbre changes when the registration switches are depressed while the manual keys are held down. Amplitude vibratos of different speeds and intensities can be produced by shaking the instrument with the hand or body while playing, and sustained pitches can be tremoloed by rapid agitation of the bellows, known to players as a "bellows shake."

The several works listed below will repay study as to the idiomatic uses of the new accordion techniques and their specialized notations:

S. Dolin: *Sonata*

T. Lundquist: *Metamorphoses; Partita Piccola,* and other works

O. Schmidt: *Toccata*

13

STRINGS

New string techniques cover a wide variety of procedures, from variants of traditional bowing and fingering patterns, pizzicato, and *sul ponticello,* to current experimentation with hybrid instruments. Though it cannot be maintained that the strings now occupy the same exalted position in the hierarchy of instruments they enjoyed in previous periods, they have by no means been relegated to positions of inferiority in the aggregate of sound-producers available to the contemporary composer. The vanguardist may not use his strings as lyric members of his ensembles, but he cannot yet do without them—as the following pages will corroborate.

Bowing devices

Experimental scores of the past several decades have displayed new and patently radical methods of employing the bow to produce string tone. The procedures discussed below, however, all have direct antecedents in past practice. The "newness" is more a question of degree than of substance, as there are, after all, only so many ways in which a bow can be held by the hand, moved with the arm, and pressed against a string.

A tight and nonrhythmicized bow-tremolo is perhaps the most prevalent among the newer bowing techniques. It has been requisitioned by far too many recent orchestrators to cite each score individually, but a glance at almost any one of Penderecki's orchestral scores will show an extensive use of the device. Parenthetically, this composer's notation, given below, is the clearest and most concise of all the many symbols devised and currently used:

An equally ubiquitous score directive today tells the players to change bow direction at will on sustained notes of long duration. In other words, uniform down-bows and up-bows are to be avoided as much as possible, thus nullifying simultaneous accent.

In the remaining contemporary bowing variants to be catalogued, the player must accomplish a number of unusual actions, such as: exert exaggerated force on the string by pressing the bow so heavily, with a twisting, grinding motion, that no precise tone but only a strident, creaking, or rasping noise is heard. This stipulation may be seen in the following works:

D. Bedford: *Five for String Quintet*

M. von Biel: *(1) Quartett*

G. Cacioppo: *Time on Time in Miracles*

A. Corghi: *Stereofonie X4*

G. Crumb: *Echoes of Time and the River*

J. Deak: *Color Studies for Contrabass* (Example 37)

J. Druckman: *Incenters; String Quartet No. 2*

D. Erb: *Concerto for Solo Percussionist; String Trio*

L. Foss: *Orpheus*

H. Gorecki: *Canti strumentali; Elementi*

C. Halffter: *Fibonaciana*

H-J. Hespos: *Passagen*

G. Heussenstamm: *Pentalogue*

J. M. Horvath: *Redundanz 2*

K. Huber: *Tenebrae*

M. Kagel: *Match; Sonant*

R. Kayn: *Galaxis*

A. Lanza: *Eidesis II*

G. Ligeti: *Nouvelles Aventures*

F. Miroglio: *Réfractions*

P. Norgård: *Symphony No. 2*

K. Penderecki: *Capriccio for Violin; De Natura Sonoris (I)*, and other works

R. Reynolds: *Quick are the Mouths of Earth*
G. Rochberg: *Tableaux*
K. E. Welin: *Nr. 3-1961*
Y. Yannay: *preFIX-FIX-sufFIX*

An interesting variant of this technique is the directive in Jack Fortner's *Quartet*: gradually raise the left-hand fingers from the strings to a position that would ordinarily produce a harmonic; at the same time, increase the bowing pressure so that recognizable pitches disintegrate into a grinding noise. On the other hand, Lejaren Hiller directs the string players in his fifth quartet to "produce a rasping grating noise by slowly dragging the bow across the strings while at the same time damping the string by pressing down on it to suppress its vibrations." And in *Charisma*, Xenakis directs the cellist to "grind on the bridge with the bow," which produces a "brutal" sound according to the composer, a description one is not inclined to question.

Other twentieth-century bowing techniques require the player to:

1. Use a rebounding bow-stroke in which pairs of notes are taken in rapid alternate up- and down-bows; known to string players as "feather bowing" or "drum stroke bowing," this technique is actually a species of ricochet (*jeté, saltando*)

   I. Stravinsky: *Le Sacre du Printemps* (see Violin I, No. 24–28)

2. Barely touch the bow-tip to the string in a sort of "lifting off" motion

   W. Sydeman: *Texture Studies*

3. Bounce the bow on the string, at the same time keeping the bow-hair tight and elastic by pressing it at the nut with the thumb

   W. Szalonek: *Concertino per flauto; Les Sons,* and other works

Example 37   Jon Deak: from *Color Studies for Contrabass* (p. 2)

4. Bounce the tip of the bow along the length of a string, a left-hand finger lightly dampening the string near the nut as though producing a harmonic. On violin and viola the bow direction is from near the bridge to close to the finger on the string; on cello (and doublebass) it is from the end of the fingerboard (below the left-hand fingers) toward the bridge

    M. Powell: *Filigree Setting* (Example 18: Violin I)

5. "Scratch" the string, using up-bow at the frog, with maximum pressure. Ordinarily, up-bow is taken at the middle or the tip of the bow, where the player has maximum control of his arm movement. To request up-bow starting at the frog gives little room in which to maneuver and creates problems of bow control, but the rough and strained quality inherent in this manner of attacking the string is precisely what the avant-gardists want

    S. Hodkinson: *Fresco*
    K. Huber: *Tenebrae*

6. Stifle a note by stopping the bow "dead" on the string, while at the same time pressing a finger down on an adjacent pitch on the same string; this technique was invented by Howard Colf, cellist in Lukas Foss's improvisation ensemble, and used in

    J. Druckman: *Incenters; String Quartet No. 2*
    L. Foss: *Echoi; Time Cycle,* and other works
    W. Sydeman: *Projections I*

7. Scrape, scratch, or glide the bow lengthwise (vertically) along the string

    W. Albright: *Danse Macabre*
    N. Castiglioni: *Eine kleine Weihnachtsmusik*
    A. Curran: *Home-made*
    J. Deak: *Color Studies for Contrabass*
    L. Hiller: *String Quartet No. 5*
    A. Hrisanide: *Volumes*
    A. Mellnäs: *Aura*
    F. Miroglio: *Projections; Réfractions*

8. Begin a down-bow at the normal distance from the bridge, gradually sliding to and over the fingerboard as the bow-stroke approaches the tip; the player then quickly and lightly returns to the bridge area with an up-bow stroke. This technique, called "circular bowing," is more feasible on cello and doublebass than on violin and viola, owing to greater string length

    M. von Biel: *(1) Quartett*
    P. Chihara: *Logs*
    J. Deak: *Color Studies for Contrabass*

9. Attack the string up-bow, the bow then moving down, rather than across, the string until the frog is reached, then returning up the string with a rapid down-bow motion; termed "eliptical bowing," the effect is possible only on cello and double-bass

   J. Deak: *Color Studies for Contrabass*

10. Bow on the string(s) with a rotating movement

    F. Miroglio: *Projections; Réfractions*

11. Bow *col legno tratto* so that an almost inaudible "whispering" scrape is heard

    P. Norgård: *Symphony No. 2*

12. Bow as close as possible to the left-hand fingers on the string(s), but on the normal side of the fingers

    L. Bassett: *Music for Cello and Piano*
    M. Kagel: *Match*

13. Bow *behind* the left-hand fingers stopping the strings (on violin or viola), or *above* the fingers on cello and doublebass

    S. Cervetti: *Zinctum*
    G. Crumb: *Eleven Echoes of Autumn; Songs, Drones, and Refrains of Death*
    J. Deak: *Color Studies for Contrabass*
    J. Fortner: *Quartet*

14. Stop the E' with just room enough for the bow between the fingers and the bridge

    D. Erb: *Concerto for Solo Percussionist*

15. Bow between the tuning pegs and the fingerboard (very near to the nut)

    S. Cervetti: *Zinctum*

16. Bow near the tuning pegs, on the "wrong" side of the left-hand fingers, the instrument (violin and viola) held like a viol and the bow also held in the manner of playing viols

    G. Crumb: *Black Angels*

17. Bow *underneath* the strings, just in front of the bridge;[1] this is most feasible, of course, on cello or doublebass

    B. Childs: *Jack's New Bag; Nonet,* and other works
    P. Méfano: *Lignes*

---

[1]Bertram Turetzky refers to this specialized technique as "reverse bowing"; inasmuch as the identical term is applied to the technique of using up-bow on accented beats and down-bow on weak beats($\lor$ $\sqcap$ rather than $\sqcap$ $\lor$), Turetzky's terminology may cause unnecessary confusion.

K. Penderecki: *Capriccio per Siegfried Palm*
P. Phillips: *Sonata for String Bass*
R. Roxbury: *Aria*

18. Play with the bow-hairs quite slack, which produces a rather pale and tenuous tone

    G. Crumb: *Songs, Drones, and Refrains of Death*

19. Strike or tap with the bow-hair on the string(s) behind the bridge

    L. Berio: *Epifanie*
    S. Cervetti: *Zinctum*
    P. Chihara: *Driftwood*
    R. Gerhard: *Epithalamium*
    A. Ginastera: *Bomarzo Cantata*
    L. Harrison: *Suite for Symphonic Strings*
    K. Huber: *Tenebrae*
    A. Lanza: *Cuarteto V*
    S. Matsushita: *Fresque sonore*
    A. Mellnäs: *Per caso*
    K. M. Nazar: *Variazioni concertanti*
    K. Penderecki: *Fluorescences; Quartetto per archi,* and other works
    A. de la Vega: *Segments for Violin and Piano; Structures for Piano and String Quartet*

20. Bow on the body of the instrument (edge of the fingerboard, the belly, or side), producing a faint, breathlike sound

    C. Alsina: *Trio 1967* (Example 22)
    V. Globokar: *Accord*
    C. Halffter: *Fibonaciana*
    K. Penderecki: *Fluorescences*
    R. M. Schafer: *Requiems for the Party-Girl*
    W. Sydeman: *Texture Studies*

21. Bow on the tailpiece; on the cello and doublebass this produces a low groaning noise

    M. von Biel: *(1) Quartett*
    E. Bujarski: *Kinoth*
    J. Deak: *Color Studies for Contrabass*
    R. L. Finney: *Percussion Concerto*
    R. Gerhard: *Concert for 8*
    V. Globokar: *Accord*
    G. Heussenstamm: *Pentalogue*
    M. Ishi: *Aphorismen*
    P. Oliveros: *Trio*

    K. Penderecki: *Capriccio per Siegfried Palm; Threnody,* and other works
    W. Szalonek: *Les Sons*

22. Bow on the string behind the tailpiece, which produces a very shrill and penetrating tone

    F. Miroglio: *Réfractions*

23. Bow on the top or side of the mute, which is placed in the normal position over the bridge

    V. Globokar: *Accord*
    C. Halffter: *Fibonaciana*

One final bowing action: it is possible to bow on the floor-peg of either the cello or the doublebass, an effect once used in a performance of Stockhausen's *Stop,* although the composer does not specify this action in his score.

It does not seem possible that further bowing variants will—or can—be devised by our avant-garde instrumentators, yet one would be rash, indeed, to make any firm prophecy. Tomorrow's new scores will doubtless handsomely repudiate even this momentary questioning.

Sul Ponticello Variants

Until about the end of the first quarter of the present century, composers utilized only one basic form of *sul ponticello.* Today there are several variant methods of employing this useful device, such as playing on the bridge itself, or on the short length of string between the bridge and the tailpiece. Each method produces a perceptible difference in timbre. When the bow is kept as close to the bridge as possible, without actually touching it, the resultant tone is dead and nasal. Although this is the manner in which authentic *sul ponticello* should be played, few players observe it without special directives such as one finds in Klaus Huber's *Alveare vernat* and in the *Filigree Setting* and *Two Prayer Settings* of Mel Powell. Quite frequently the stipulation is coupled with a request to play nonvibrato, which further enhances the disembodied color of *sul ponticello.*

Playing directly over the bridge (on the string) results in a buzzing sound rather than any identifiable pitch. Some of the composers who have asked for this effect include:

    B. Bartolozzi: *Quartetto per archi*
    D. Bedford: *Five for String Quintet; That White and Radiant Legend*

L. Berio: *Sincronie*
M. von Biel: *(1) Quartett*
A. Boucourechliev: *Archipel II*
J. Deak: *Color Studies for Contrabass*
V. Globokar: *Accord*
H-J. Hespos: *Passagen*
A. Hrisanide: *Volumes*
M. Kagel: *Match*
R. Kayn: *Galaxis*
W. Kilar: *Riff 62*
M. Kopelent: *3. Quartetto*
A. Lanza: *Cuarteto V*
B. J. Layton: *Divertimento*
G. Ligeti: *Aventures; Cello Concerto*
K. Penderecki: *Fluorescences*
R. Reynolds: *Quick are the Mouths of Earth*
W. Sydeman: *Projections I*
E. Valcarcel: *Dicotomia III*

A few composers have also directed their string players to strike the strings directly over the bridge with the heel of the bow, producing a rough and rasping noise:

B. Bartolozzi: *Quartetto per archi*
S. Cervetti: *Zinctum*
A. Lanza: *Cuarteto V*

It is possible, although rather awkward, to bow on the bridge of the cello or doublebass without touching the strings, accomplished by the player's holding the bow parallel to the strings (requested in Roger Reynolds' *Quick are the Mouths of Earth*). On all the string members the players may bow on the side of the bridge; on violin and viola this manner of bowing creates a faint hissing, while on cello and doublebass it produces a kind of high-pitched groan. Refer to:

M. von Biel: *(1) Quartett*
D. Cope: *Angel's Camp II* (Example 38)
J. Deak: *Color Studies for Contrabass; Surrealist Studies*
M. Mitrea-Celarianu: *Seth*
K. Penderecki: *The Devils of Loudun; Polymorphia,* and other works
B. Rands: *Memo 1*
K. Stockhausen: *Mixtur*

Example 38   David Cope: from *Angel's Camp II* (p. 6)

Playing with the bow-hair on the strings behind the bridge has become one of the most ubiquitous bowing requirements to be found in current vanguard scores. No precise pitch is obtainable, of course, on the very short length of string in that area, but only an indefinite squeaking sound. The glassy edge to the sounds normally associated with *sul ponticello* is thus even further magnified. A casual perusal of almost any score of the Polish avant-gardists, in particular those of Penderecki, will amply illustrate the technique.

A commonly utilized facet of this new instrumental procedure is to arpeggiate the bow across the four strings (or over only two or three) between the bridge and tailpiece, creating a rustling metallic sussuration, as in Hans Werner Henze's *Sinfonia N. 6* (Example 39). Although Penderecki must be accorded credit for inventing the following pictorial and highly pragmatic notation:

the device is used almost excessively in various of his scores. One should be well aware that this unique technique can rather easily wear out its welcome.

There is little room to maneuver the bow on the strings behind the bridge, yet Michael von Biel in his first string quartet specifies that the player's bow should operate closer to the tailpiece in one instance and nearer to the bridge in another. On cello and doublebass, of course, the player has considerably more string length back of the bridge and thus is able to make a greater distinction between keeping the bow close to the bridge area or to the tailpiece itself.

A further refinement of beyond-the-bridge playing is stipulated in Sydney Hodkinson's orchestral *Fresco:* the bow is to be gradually moved from close to or actually atop the bridge proper to behind it. The reverse effect is also feasible, the bow moving from near the tailpiece to or beyond the bridge on the fingerboard side; so far this stipulation has eluded discovery in any contemporary score.

Curious directives are almost commonplace in avant-garde works, but one of the most intriguing appears in the Israeli composer Yizhak Sadai's *Nuances:* the violins are told to play behind the bridge with a pocket comb—an effect that is quite impossible to describe.

Directly related to these *sul ponticello* refinements just described are the techniques of bouncing the bow, *saltato,* or *jeté,* from over the fingerboard toward or literally over the bridge, or in the reverse direction, from bridge to fingerboard. Some of the recent works requesting these allied techniques include:

I. Anhalt: *Foci* (Example 15)
L. Berio: *Sincronie*

Example 39   Hans Werner Henze: from *Sinfonia N. 6* (p. 81)

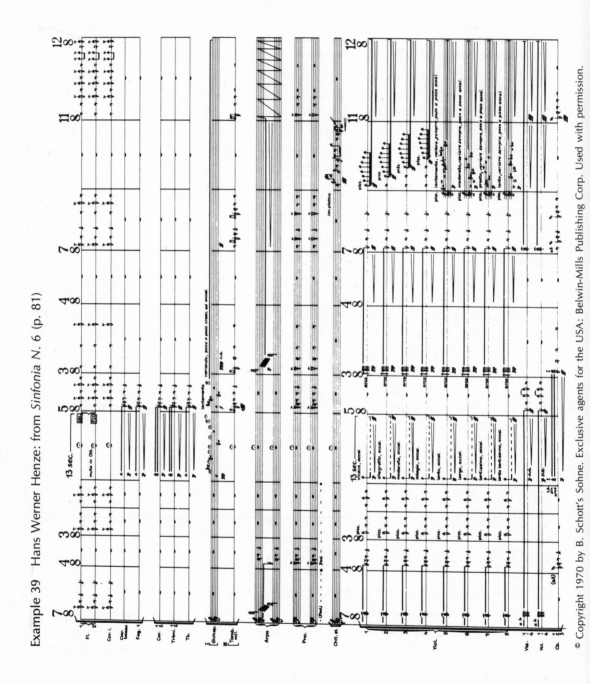

B. Childs: *Nonet*
M. Colgrass: *As Quiet As*
J. Druckman: *Incenters; String Quartet No. 2*
M. Kopelent: *3. Quartetto*
R. Reynolds: *Quick are the Mouths of Earth*

Also the bow can be made to move slowly, often in tremolo, from the bridge area to over the fingerboard, close to the left-hand fingers on the strings; see:

L. Bassett: *Music for Cello and Piano*
E. Brown: *Available Forms 2; String Quartet*
L. Foss: *Elytres*
R. Haubenstock-Ramati: *Séquences*
M. Kagel: *Heterophonie*
G. Ligeti: *Aventures; Cello Concerto*
G. Read: *Symphony No. 3*
W. Sydeman: *Projections I*
V. Wagenheim: *Klangspiel I*
L. Widdoes: *From a Time of Snow*

The reverse procedure—moving with the bow from high on the fingerboard, or from normal position, toward the bridge or beyond it—is equally feasible and as frequently requested:

J. Cage: *26'1.1499" for a String Player*
D. Erb: *Basspiece*
M. Kagel: *Sexteto de cuerdas; Sonant*
R. M. Schafer: *String Quartet*

Rapid-fire alternations between the extremes of *sul ponticello* and *sul tasto*—or between string attacks in normal position and in the fingerboard or bridge areas—are also feasible, though admittedly difficult of control. The technique, needless to say, is highly regarded by our present composers. This coloristic concept has also been extended to comprise all manners of sound production on the various stringed instruments. Hence, one frequently finds notational or verbal instructions to the player to alternate rapidly between arco techniques—in normal position, on the bridge, over the fingerboard, in harmonics, and so on—and pizzicato (snap, behind the bridge, with the nail, glissandi, and the like) and *col legno*, either on the strings, the tailpiece, or other areas of the instrument body. These requirements are well illustrated in the following works:

E. Brown: *String Quartet*
S. Fisher: *Concert Piece*
B. Rands: *Wildtrack 1*

An exaggerated *sul ponticello* action in which the player presses the bow-hair against the mute in its usual position atop the bridge is a technical feature of Jacob Druckman's second string quartet. Not only is the timbre drastically altered by this action but the pitch is obscured as well.

Fingering Effects

To make a virtue out of a necessity is a maxim that often applies to avant-garde instrumentational experimentation. A clear case in point is the utilization of string instrument fingering action without the customary accompanying bow-strokes. In other words, the player is asked to finger audibly a series of notated pitches (or to follow the contour of a sequence of approximate pitches suggested by a series of note-stems minus note-heads). In either case, the bow is not brought into play on the strings. The aural result of this action is a faint and delicate rustling, a percussive quality both illusive and provocative. A great many composers have requested this technique, among them the following:

W. Albright: *Danse Macabre*
D. Bedford: *Five for String Quintet; That White and Radiant Legend*
A. Boucourechliev: *Archipel II*
F. Cerha: *Relazioni fragili*
B. Childs: *Nonet*
G. Crumb: *Madrigals—I*
M. Davidovsky: *Synchronisms No. 3*
A. Dobrowolski: *Music for String Orchestra*
J. Fortner: *Quartet*
L. Foss: *Baroque Variations; Echoi,* and other works
S. Hodkinson: *Fresco*
A. Hrisanide: *Volumes*
M. Kagel: *Match; Sonant*
E. Karkoschka: *Quattrologe*
M. Kelemen: *Changeant; Surprise*
G. Ligeti: *Apparitions; Ramifications,* and other works
K. Penderecki: *Capriccio per Siegfried Palm; Emanationen,* and other works
G. Read: *Villon*
D. Reck: *Blues and Screamer*

R. Reynolds: *Quick are the Mouths of Earth*
W. Sydeman: *Texture Studies*
I. Yun: *String Quartet No. 3*

Equally effective in sound is an audible roll or tremolo on one string with two left-hand fingers, as in:

N. Castiglioni: *A Solemn Music II*
A. Hrisanide: *Volumes*
M. Kupferman: *Infinities 24*
E. Kurtz: *Improvisation for Contrabass*
K. Penderecki: *Quartetto per archi*
B. Schäffer: *Scultura; String Quartet*

In Charles Whittenberg's *Conversations* for solo doublebass, the composer specifies a finger-roll on an open string gradually going into a fingered pitch; two fingers alternately trill on the string while a third finger slowly presses down on it.

A drumlike roll using from two to four fingers on two adjacent strings is most feasible on the larger stringed instruments, cello and doublebass, as, for instance, in:

G. Crumb: *Madrigals—I*
B. A. Zimmermann: *Sonate für Cello Solo*

Loud fingering action can also be combined with certain bowing procedures: in *Blues and Screamer,* for example, David Reck stipulates that the bow be used very lightly, producing a barely audible tone while at the same time the left-hand fingers strongly finger the designated pitches. A more delicately articulated fingering, coupled with very light bowing pressure, is several times requested by Boguslaw Schäffer in his *Two Pieces* for violin and piano.

Another ramification of this technique is to gradually stop the bow action but continue the perceptible fingerings of the notated pitches (as in Ligeti's cello concerto). Ordinarily, the fingertips are used for audible fingerings, but the nails may also be specified. In Ligeti's *Aventures,* for example, the composer instructs the solo doublebass player: "With the fingernails travel delicately, very slowly and aperiodically along the strings."

A finger-roll is combined with *sul ponticello* bowing on the same string in Barry Brosch's *Prolations,* and in *Valentine* of Jacob Druckman the solo bassist is asked to bring a finger down on an open string so hard that the string resonates.

Several unorthodox fingering actions are featured in Luciano Berio's virtuoso *Sequenza VI* for solo viola (and related *Chemins II*). For example: the
fingers are to be shifted randomly in both a wide and a minimal distance from
the necessary position to sound a given four-note structure, creating a highly
unstable frequency situation. For wide shiftings the finger-slides must, of
course, be in the same direction on the four strings; for minute shiftings the
slides may actually be in contrary motion. A further directive in Berio's score is
to alternate as quickly as possible the normal and the harmonic positions of the
fingers on all four strings; that is, to press down firmly with the fingers and then
to raise them so that they only lightly touch on the strings, as at a harmonic
node.

In *The Seventh Trumpet*, Donald Erb directs the string players to finger
with the left hand between the fingerboard and the bridge while plucking the
strings over the fingerboard —a reversal of the normal relative positions of left-
and right-hand fingers.

Pizzicato Variants

Pizzicato was the first of a long historical succession of unorthodox techniques applied to bowed stringed instruments. From its first appearance in
Claudio Monteverdi's *Il Combattimento di Tancredi e Clorinda* of 1607, however, up to the closing years of the nineteenth century, pizzicato was basically a
one-dimensional device. That is to say, pizzicato meant simply to pluck the
string with the tip of the right-hand index finger. Pizzicato with the left hand,
which was introduced into solo literature for the strings in the seventeenth
century, enabled the player concurrently to pluck and bow the strings. Pizzicato
on natural harmonics, extensively used in late nineteenth century orchestration by such composers as Rimsky-Korsakov, Mahler, and Debussy, for example, was only an extension of the basic technique and did not radically alter the
generic timbre of pizzicato.

As the late Romantic instrumentators became more and more preoccupied
with instrumental tone color and unusual sonorities, pizzicato gradually
acquired certain notable variant forms, both in manners of production and in
resultant sound. Thus such effects as are listed below were common coinage
among orchestrators during the earliest years of the present century:

1. Pizzicato tremolando (or "banjo" pizzicato), the strings rapidly strummed with the
   forefinger (or several fingers) of the right hand, as in Sir Edward Elgar's *Violin
   Concerto,* for instance. Contemporary examples would include almost any composition of Alan Hovhaness using the strings, and refer also to

R. Erickson: *Ricercar à 3*
E. Karkoschka: *Quattrologe*
B. Kolb: *Trobar Clus*

2. "Reverse" pizzicato, the four strings plucked in the direction opposite to that normally employed (*i.e.*, down for violin and viola, up for cello and doublebass)

3. "Guitar" or "brush" pizzicato (or pizzicato arpeggiato), the strings gently stroked with the thumb or several fingers; recent examples include

B. Bartolozzi: *Quartetto per archi*
J. Deak: *Color Studies for Contrabass*
H. Dianda: *Estructuras*
G. Heussenstamm: *Pentalogue*
H. Pousseur: *Ode pour quatour à cordes*
B. Rands: *Memo 1*
C. Whittenberg: *Conversations for Solo Double Bass*
I. Xenakis: *Nomos*

4. Pizzicato glissando, the string(s) plucked and then the left hand sliding quickly along the string, as in Stravinsky's *Renard* and numerous scores of Bartók; current examples are almost astronomical in number

5. "Pinch" pizzicato, the string plucked with two fingers rather than only one; early examples may be found in a number of Stravinsky scores, such as the *Concertino for String Quartet* and *Ragtime*, also in Bartók's *First Rhapsody* and the *Kammersymphonie I* of Schoenberg. More recent usages include

J. Deak: *Color Studies for Contrabass*
G. Ligeti: *Aventures*
S. Matsushita: *Fresque sonore*
W. Szalonek: *Concertino per flauto*
R. Wittinger: *Construzioni*

6. "Snap" or "slap" pizzicato, 'a la Bartók, evidently first used in the Scherzo movement of Mahler's seventh symphony; it is now too common to warrant individual citations of current works

By the mid-point of the present century pizzicato effects had further proliferated; to the standardized variants just listed we must now add the following:

1. "Plectrum" pizzicato, the string plucked with a guitar, mandolin, or banjo pick

B. Childs: *Mr. T., His Fancy*
G. Crumb: *Night of the Four Moons*
F. Evangelisti: *Aleatorio*

L. Hiller: *String Quartet No. 5*
M. Kelemen: *Changeant*
W. Kilar: *Dipthongos*
W. Szalonek: *Les Sons; Proporzioni II*

2. Pizzicato "al mandolino," a variant of the above; the instrument (violin or viola only) is held like a mandolin and the strings are strummed rapidly with a plectrum
   B. Childs: *Nonet*
   G. Crumb: *Eleven Echoes of Autumn*
   H. Pousseur: *Ode pour quatour à cordes*
   B. Rands: *Wildtrack 1*
   W. Sydeman: *Texture Studies*

3. Pizzicato with a nail-file, another variant of the "plectrum pizzicato," and designated in Frank Beyer's *Versi*

The fingernails are sometimes designated as a substitute for a pick. A tremolando on a single string of either cello or doublebass can be likewise effectuated with a plectrum or the nails, as in Charles Whittenberg's *Conversations*.

4. "Nut" pizzicato, the string lightly plucked not with the finger but with the nut of the bow, with a lifting motion, creating a delicate click; requested by Sergio Cervetti in his *Zinctum*

5. "Bisbigliando" pizzicato, the four fingers of the right hand rapidly and alternately plucking a single string; the delicate drumming sound so produced was requisitioned by Bernd Alois Zimmermann in his solo cello sonata

6. "Pulled" pizzicato, a variant of snap pizzicato on cello and doublebass; the lowest string is pulled to the side of the fingerboard as it is plucked, rebounding against the fingerboard when it is released (see Jacob Druckman's *Valentine*)

7. "Hammer on" pizzicato, an open string being plucked and the note a semitone higher immediately and forcefully fingered, thus abruptly stifling the string's vibration
   B. Childs: *Mr. T., His Fancy*
   T. Frederickson: *Music for Five Instruments*

8. Pizzicato "effleuré," the left-hand finger placed lightly on the string as it is plucked so that an indefinite rather than a precise pitch is produced
   F. Cerha: *Formation et Solution*
   G. Ligeti: *Apparitions*

9. "Muffled" pizzicato, the outer edge of the right hand pressing down on the string(s) near the bridge as the fingers pluck the string(s), giving the pizzicato a very dull and dry sound

   G. Heussenstamm: *Pentalogue*
   W. Kotonski: *Pour quatre*

10. "Silent" pizzicato, the string actually not plucked but lightly knocked or flicked with the right-hand index finger so that a very soft and delicate click is heard; this was requested in *Dicotomia III* of Edgar Valcarcel.

Although the "nail" pizzicato is no longer novel, having been used by Bartók as early as 1936 (in the *Music for Strings, Percussion and Celesta*), it is more prevalent in current scores than most of the other variant forms of pizzicato previously listed. Furthermore, there are at least eight different ways in which nail pizzicati may be utilized:

1. The string is plucked with an upward motion of the right-hand second fingernail, the most common method of employing the technique (as in the Bartók work just cited)

2. The string is plucked with the nail quite close to the bridge, which imparts an even greater metallic and brittle quality to the sound

   J. M. Horvath: *Redundanz 2*
   W. Sydeman: *Study for Orchestra No. III*

3. The upper nail surface is placed underneath the string, which is then plucked with a rapid upward motion of the finger; consult the *Five Pieces from Mikrokosmos* of Bartók, arranged by Tibor Serly

4. The string is plucked in a normal manner but is allowed to vibrate against the fingernail of the plucking finger; termed "buzz" pizzicato, the device has been used by

   E. Brown: *Music for Cello and Piano*
   E. Carter: *String Quartet No. 2*
   F. Cerha: *Enjambments; Formation et Solution*
   H-J. Hespos: *Passagen*
   M. Kagel: *Sonant*
   M. Kelemen: *Changeant*
   G. Ligeti: *Apparitions*
   P. Oliveros: *Trio*
   B. Rands: *Memo 1*
   I. Xenakis: *ST/4-1, 080262*

5. After the string is normally plucked, the right-hand finger is turned over and slowly removed from the string so that the nail surface buzzes against the vibrating string (see Mauricio Kagel's *Sonant*)

6. The left-hand fingernail is placed lightly on the string to be plucked, just barely touching it, so that the plucked string will vibrate against the nail tip

   F. Cerha: *Enjambments; Formation et Solution*
   D. Martino: *Fantasy-Variations*

7. The string is plucked normally and then the left-hand fingernail lightly touches the already vibrating string

   J. Druckman: *Valentine*
   I. Xenakis: *ST/4-1, 080262*

8. The string is tightened by pulling it with the right-hand fingernail while at the same time the left hand plucks the string

   I. Yun: *Dimensionen*

The foregoing list by no means exhausts the diversities of pizzicato to be found in recent scores of an experimental nature. Among the remaining specialized pizzicato effects are the following:

1. Normal pizzicato behind the bridge, which produces a dull and relatively unpitched sound; almost any string composition by Kagel, Ligeti, Penderecki, Serocki, for example, will provide ample demonstration of this technique

2. Pizzicato behind the bridge with the fingernail (see, for instance, R. M. Schafer's *String Quartet*); in Donald Erb's *Concerto for Solo Percussionist* the players of the lower-pitched strings are asked to stroke rapidly on the strings beyond the bridge with the nails

3. Pizzicato behind the bridge with a guitar pick

   D. Cope: *Angel's Camp II* (Example 38)
   L. Harrison: *Suite for Symphonic Strings*

4. Pizzicato with the left-hand finger lightly touching the string, like a half-harmonic, but *not* at a harmonic node

   F. Cerha: *Enjambments; Formation et Solution*
   G. Ligeti: *Apparitions*
   I. Yun: *Colloides sonores*

5. Left-hand pizzicato and arco on the same string simultaneously

   H. Dianda: *Estructuras*
   A. Lanza: *Cuarteto V; Eidesis II*
   D. Reck: *Blues and Screamer*

6. Pizzicato rapidly alternating with arco on a single pitch, quasi-tremolo

   D. Bedford: *Trona*

7. Left-hand pizzicato and *col legno* simultaneously

   L. Berio: *Sequenza VI*
   S. Cervetti: *Zinctum*
   M. Kagel: *Match*

8. A slow and measured arpeggiated pizzicato in which the right-hand finger stretches each string before releasing it, similar to the "pulled" pizzicato described on page 222; this manner of plucking was utilized by Henri Pousseur in his *Ode pour quatour à cordes*

9. Dampen the string by pressing down on it with the left-hand finger, then snap the string forcefully, à la Bartók

   K. Huber: *Alveare vernat*
   G. Ligeti: *Apparitions*
   M. Mamiya: *String Quartet No. 1*

10. Pizzicato like guitar harmonics; the left-hand finger is lifted off the string immediately after the string is plucked, causing the tone to ring in a clear manner; see *Eleven Echoes of Autumn* and *Echoes of Time and the River* by George Crumb

11. "Bottle-neck" pizzicato, the string plucked with a plectrum or paper clip while the left hand holds a small glass rod which is slid along the string to produce a series of portamento pitches (called for in these same two compositions)

12. Pizzicato on various specified parts of the string, ranging from near the pegs or nut to close to or beyond the bridge

    L. Ferrari: *Société II* (Example 40)
    G. Heussenstamm: *Pentalogue*

13. Pizzicato on the strings (of doublebass) *above* the left-hand fingers on the fingerboard; requested in *Memo 1* by Bernard Rands

14. Pizzicato on the string area in the peg-box (of doublebass)

    J. Deak: *Surrealist Studies*

Example 40 Luc Ferrari: from *Société II* (p. 6)

226

Not a pizzicato variant, yet an effect that depends on the fingernail, is the directive in *Match* (for cello) of Kagel to place a nail next to or underneath the string to be played arco, so that a jangling noise is heard. And in Sergio Cervetti's *Six Sequences*, the cellist is instructed to place his left-hand thumbnail on the string near to the bridge while playing arco, which produces the same general effect.

Miscellaneous Effects

A compositional rather than a strictly idiomatic technique is the prevalent use of massed string clusters, yet significant enough in contemporary orchestration to warrant inclusion here. Sustained clusters are generally indicated as shown at the left below, each pitch assumed by one player in the section. As devised by Penderecki, the notation at the right calls for each player to trill on his designated pitch:

A technique limited to the larger instruments—cello and doublebass—and known to players as the "tambourine rub" is accomplished by the player's pressing his thumb hard against the front of the instrument (the belly) and rubbing it to produce a coarse frictional sound (see G. Heussenstamm: *Pentalogue*).

Finally, just as the wind and brass instruments have utilized the principle of sympathetic vibration by directing their tones into the interior of a grand piano (see page 160), so have the strings (violin and viola only) occasionally capitalized on this available modern resource (Penderecki's *Miniatures* for violin and piano, for example). More suited to chamber music than to symphonic requirements, this effect is auditory and visual in almost equal proportions.

Hybrid Instruments

Although major improvements in construction and minor refinements in detail have been applied to nearly all of the woodwind and brass instruments during the present and last centuries, the strings—individually and collectively—have undergone no such development. Quite recently, however, there have been attempts, motivated scientifically as well as musically, to redesign the family of bowed string instruments. In so doing, the aim has been to produce a more homogeneous sound from bottom to top of the total string gamut and to create a far greater dynamic range than now exists among massed violins, violas, violoncellos, and doublebasses.

The traditional format of the symphonic string section has long demonstrated a wide discrepancy between the timbres of doublebass and of violin. Furthermore, despite its size and the length of its strings in relation to the violin, the doublebass does not produce a correlated increase in amplitude. It is primarily to rectify these tonal and dynamic discrepancies that the Catgut Acoustical Society of America has recently fostered the development of eight new instruments, scaled to basic violin design and to its general tonal characteristics. Thus, the new family of stringed instruments is capable of creating a timbral and a dynamic consistency between all its members, a not inconsiderable achievement.

Whether these conditions are considered as musical virtues by all composers is debatable. The criteria of certain artistic philosophies currently in high favor do not regard tonal homogeneity and dynamic equality as desirable goals. Other, and equally viable viewpoints, however, will look upon these conditions as distinct musical advantages. At any rate, whatever the philosophical point of view, new and demonstrably useful string instruments are now a reality and are available, even if in a severely limited way, to orchestrators interested in enlarging their string instrument resources.

CODA

It is unlikely that the current widespread, almost frenetic, experimentation with instrumental devices and sonoric effects will soon slacken in pace. There will inevitably be further refinements of existing techniques, whether recently devised or long in common use. Additional multiphonic structures for the woodwinds, for instance, will be discovered; new percussive effects on brass, keyboard, and stringed instruments will be exploited; other bizarre instruments will be introduced into the percussion section of the orchestra; newly designed or hybrid instruments will take their place in the existing instrumental families in the avant-garde scores of the years just ahead. For the twentieth century has been—and will continue to be—a time when composers of all stylistic persuasions are augmenting their sound resources, humanly performed or electronically generated.

In the future, there may well be a more equalized application of new techniques among all the instrumental choirs. At the moment, some instruments (the piano, for instance) have been perhaps overexploited in the application of new and unorthodox effects; others (the horn, for one) have not been as intensely explored. Some vanguardists may come to realize that many novel devices are simply not worth the effort involved in producing them. Either the timbre distinctions created by the unusual techniques are so minute as to be virtually imperceptible, or they are so inordinately difficult and physically awkward to produce that they cannot really be regarded as compositionally legitimate.

One cannot, of course, confidently predict where the search for novel instrumental and vocal effect will ultimately lead today's composers and orchestrators, but one can hope that the present more limited focus on external means will eventually grow into a wider vision of expressive ends. Meanwhile, the search for new devices, new notations, new sounds, new techniques will continue, as it must.

ACKNOWLEDGMENTS

Books are customarily dedicated to persons, living or dead, and seldom to inanimate objects. This book, however, is dedicated to a ship: the Norwegian freighter *Tagaytay,* on which I enjoyed an extended trip to the Far East in 1972. Between exotic ports of call—Manila, Singapore, Kuala Lumpur, Belewan, Hong Kong, Taipei, Pusan, Yokohama,—this survey of contemporary instrumental techniques took concrete shape. In welcome privacy and tacitly encouraged by discreet ship's personnel and understanding fellow passengers, voluminous notes were transformed into organized chapters and unfocused thoughts and impressions were honed into specific observation and critical commentary.

In addition, I am, in a more conventional though no less sincere literary manner, deeply appreciative of valuable assistance from the following individuals: Robert Dick, John C. Heiss, and James Pellerite for the latest information on multiphonics and other new wind instrument techniques; Milton Stevens for systematic and thorough demonstration of recent brass instrument devices; Gary Washburn for up-to-date matters relating to the saxophone family; Richard Romiti for authoritative explanation of the modern free-bass accordion technique, and Carleen M. Hutchins of the Catgut Acoustical Society for data on some newly designed string instruments.

A special word of appreciation goes to Arthur Daniels and Nicolas Slonimsky for detailed criticism of the manuscript and for many valuable suggestions for its improvement. I am also greatly indebted to the Graduate School of Boston University for a faculty grant-in-aid that enabled me to complete the book sooner than anticipated.

Kindest thanks are also due the following publishers' representatives for their cooperation in making available recent and appropriate publications: Alfred Blatter (Media Press), David Cope (Composers' Autograph Publications), Stephen Fisher (C. F. Peters Corporation), Robert Holton (Belwin-Mills Publishing Corp.), Henson Markham (Editions Salabert), Eugene Moon (Theodore Presser Company), Barry O'Neal (Associated Music Publishers), Stuart W. Pope (Boosey & Hawkes, Inc.), Raoul R. Ronson (Seesaw Music Corp.), and Elliott Schwartz (Bowdoin College Music Press). The directors of Moeck Verlag and of G. Ricordi & Co. also provided me with invaluable materials, for which sincere appreciation is expressed.

Acknowledgment is hereby extended to the following publishers for granting permission to use excerpts from publications under their control: Associated Music Publishers, Inc. (for Bote & Bock, Aldo Bruzzichelli, and G. Schirmer, Inc.); Belwin-Mills Publishing Corp. (for Moeck Verlag and B. Schott's Sohne); Berandol Music Ltd.; Boosey & Hawkes, Inc.; Bowdoin College Music Press; M. M. Cole Publishing Co.; M.C.A. Music; Media Press, Inc.; C. F. Peters Corporation (for Henmar Press, Inc. and Henry Litolff's Verlag); Polskie Wydawnictwo Muzyczne; Theodore Presser Company (for Universal Edition); Editions Salabert; E. C. Schirmer Music Co.; Seesaw Music Corp.; Shawnee Press, Inc., Source—Music of the Avant-Garde.

BIBLIOGRAPHY

BARTOLOZZI, BRUNO. *New Sounds for Woodwind.* London: Oxford University Press, 1967.

BLADES, JAMES. *Percussion Instruments and their History* (Chapter 15: *Techniques of Contemporary Percussion;* Chapter 16: *Composers' Use of Modern Percussion*). New York: Frederick A. Praeger, Publishers, 1970.

BRANT, HENRY. "Space as an Essential Aspect of Musical Composition," in *Contemporary Composers on Contemporary Music,* edited by Barney Childs and Elliott Schwartz. New York: Holt, Rinehart and Winston, 1967.

BRINDLE, REGINALD SMITH. *Contemporary Percussion.* London: Oxford University Press, 1970.

BROOKS, WILLIAM. "Instrumental and Vocal Resources," in *Dictionary of Contemporary Music,* edited by John Vinton. New York: E. P. Dutton & Co., Inc., 1974.

BUNGER, RICHARD. *The Well-Prepared Piano.* Colorado Springs: Colorado College Music Press, 1973.

COPE, DAVID. *New Directions in Music.* Dubuque: Wm. C. Brown Company Publishers, 1971.

DICK, ROBERT. *The Other Flute: A Performance Manual of Contemporary Techniques.* London: Oxford University Press, 1974.

HEISS, JOHN C. "For the Flute: A List of Double-Stops, Triple-Stops, Quadruple-Stops and Shakes." Princeton: *Perspectives of New Music,* Vol. 5, No. 1, 1966.

——"Some Multiple Sonorities for Flute, Oboe, Clarinet, and Bassoon." Princeton: *Perspectives of New Music.* Vol. 7, No. 1, 1968.

——"The Flute: New Sounds." Princeton: *Perspectives of New Music,* Vol. 11, No. 1, 1972.

HOWELL, THOMAS. *The Avant-Garde Flute*. Berkeley: University of California Press, 1974.

PELLERITE, JAMES J. *A Modern Guide to Fingerings for the Flute*. Bloomington: Zalo Publications, 1972.

READ, GARDNER. *Thesaurus of Orchestral Devices*. Westport: Greenwood Press, Inc., 1969 (New York: Pitman Publishing Co., 1953).

SALZEDO, CARLOS. *Modern Study of the Harp*. New York: G. Schirmer, Inc., 1921.

SMITH, WILLIAM O. "Contemporary Clarinet Sonorities." Elkhart: *Selmer Bandwagon*, No. 67, 1973.

STOKES, SHERIDON and RICHARD CONDON. *Special Effects for Flute*. Culver City: Trio Associates, 1970.

STONE, KURT. "The Piano and the Avant-Garde." New York: *The Piano Quarterly*, No. 52, 1965.

TEAL, LARRY. *The Art of Saxophone Playing*. Evanston: Summy-Birchard Company, 1963.

TURETZKY, BERTRAM. "The Bass as a Drum." Cleveland: *The Composer*, Vol. 1, No. 2, 1969.

———. *The Contemporary Contrabass*. Berkeley: University of California Press, 1974.

———. "A Technique of Contemporary Writing for the Contrabass." Cleveland: *The Composer*, Vol. 1, No. 3, 1969.

VARIOUS AUTHORS. "New Directions in Instrumental Music." Evanston: *The Instrumentalist*, Vol. XXVIII, No. 10, 1974.

VERKOEYEN, JOS. "String-Players and New Music." Amsterdam: *Sonorum Speculum*, No. 45, 1970.

Index

INDEX OF INSTRUMENTAL
REFERENCE

INDEX OF COMPOSERS
AND WORKS

LIST OF PUBLISHERS

AHN: Ahn & Simrock, Berlin (AMP)
AMPH: Amphion-Editions Musicales, Paris (B/M)
APOG: Apogee Press, Cincinnati (WLSM)
ARMP: Arrow Music Press, Inc., New York (AMP)
AVV: Ars Viva Verlag, Mainz (B/M)
AMP: Associated Music Publishers, Inc., New York
AXP: Axelrod Publications, Inc., Providence (SHP)
BAR: Bärenreiter-Verlag, Kassel (B/M)
B/M: Belwin/Mills Publishing Corp., Melville, N.Y.
BDOL: Berandol Music, Ltd., Scarborough, Ontario
BER: Edizioni Musicali Berben, Ancona, Italy (TP)
BMIC: BMI Canada, Ltd., Don Mills (AMP)
BOON: Joseph Boonin, Inc., South Hackensack, N. J.
BH: Boosey & Hawkes, Inc., New York; London
B&B: Bote & Bock, Berlin (AMP)
BOW: Bowdoin College Music Press, Brunswick, Maine
BR&H: Breitkopf & Härtel, Leipzig (AMP)
AB: Alexander Broude, Inc., New York
BRUZ: Edizioni Aldo Bruzzichelli, Florence (AMP)
CHAP: Chappell & Co., Ltd., London; New York
CHES: J. and W. Chester, Ltd., London (GS)
COLE: M. M. Cole Publishing Co., Chicago
COLF: Colfranc Music Publishing Corp., New York (B/M)
FCOL: Franco Colombo Publications, New York (B/M)
CPE: Composer-Performer Edition, Sacramento
CAP: Composers' Autograph Publications, Hamilton, Ohio
DOB: Verlag Doblinger, Vienna (AMP)
DON: Donemus, Amsterdam (CFP)
DUR: Edition Durand, Paris (EV)
ESCH: Editions Max Eschig, Paris (AMP)
EUL: Ernst Eulenberg, Ltd., London (CFP)
EV: Elkan-Vogel, Inc., Bryn Mawr (TP)
CF: Carl Fischer, Inc., New York
GAL: Galaxy Music Corp., New York

GEN: General Music Publishing Co., Hastings-on-Hudson, N.Y.
WH: Wilhelm Hansen Edition, Copenhagen (AB)
HAN: Hänssler-Verlag, Stuttgart (CFP)
HEUG: Heugel & Cie., Paris (TP)
HIGT: Highgate Press, Inc., New York (GAL)
HIN: Hinrichsen Edition, Ltd., London (CFP)
HOH: Matth. Hohner A. G., Musikverlag, Trossingen
IMPR: Impero Verlag, Wilhelmshaven (TP)
INT: International Music Co., London
IMP: Israeli Music Publications, Ltd., Tel Aviv (MCA)
JJ: Editions Jean Jobert, Paris (EV)
LG: Lawson-Gould Music Publishers, Inc., New York (GS)
LEED: Leeds Music Corp., New York (MCA)
LIT: Henry Litolff's Verlag, Frankfurt (CFP)
LYRA: Lyra Music Co., New York
MAL: Malcolm Music, Ltd., New York (SHP)
MS: Manuscript (contact composer)
EBM: Edward B. Marks Music Corp., New York (B/M)
MCA: MCA Music, New York (B/M)
MMX: McGinnis & Marx, New York
MP: Media Press, Champaign, Ill.
MER: Merion Music, Inc., Bryn Mawr (TP)
MIL: Mills Music, Inc., New York (B/M)
EMOD: Edition Modern, Munich
MV: Moeck-Verlag, Celle, Germany (B/M)
MUZ: Editura Muzicala, Bucharest
NME: New Music Edition, New York (TP)
NORD: Nordiska Musikforlaget, Stockholm
NOV: Novello & Co., Ltd., London (B/M)
ONT: Ongaku-no-Tomo Sha, Inc., Tokyo (TP)
OUP: Oxford University Press, London; New York
PAU: Pan American Union, Washington, D.C. (SMP)
CFP: C. F. Peters Corporation, New York
PHIL: Philharmonia Partituren, Vienna (BOON)
PWM: Polskie Wydawnictwo Muzycne, Cracow (EBM)
TP: Theodore Presser Co., Bryn Mawr
RIC: G. Ricordi & C., Milan (B/M)
SAL: Editions Salabert, Paris; New York
SAM: Samfundet til udgivelse af dansk musik, Copenhagen
ECS: E. C. Schirmer Music Co., Boston
GS: G. Schirmer, Inc., New York
SCHM: B. Schott's Söhne, Mainz (B/M)
SCHL: Schott & Co., Ltd., London (B/M)
SEE: Seesaw Music Corp., New York
SEN: Edition Maurice Senart, Paris (SAL)
SHP: Shawnee Press, Inc., Delaware Water Gap, Pa.
SMP: Southern Music Publishing Co., New York
TON: Edition Tonos, Darmstadt
TRI: Tritone Press, Bryn Mawr (TP)

UE: Universal Edition, A.G., Vienna; London (BOON)
UCP: University of California Press, Berkeley
WAT: Waterloo Music Co., Ltd., Waterloo, Ontario
WEIN: Josef Weinberger, Ltd., London (BH)
WLSM: World Library of Sacred Music, Cincinnati
ZER: Edizioni Suvini Zerboni, Milan (MCA)